H. James

Henry Adams.

The Correspondence of
Henry James and Henry Adams

# The Correspondence of
# Henry James and
# Henry Adams, 1877–1914

Edited, with an Introduction, by George Monteiro

LOUISIANA STATE UNIVERSITY PRESS    Baton Rouge and London

Copyright © 1992 by Louisiana State University Press
All rights reserved
Manufactured in the United States of America
01 00 99 98 97 96 95 94 93 92     5 4 3 2 1

Designer: Glynnis Phoebe
Typeface: Bembo
Typesetter: Graphic Composition, Inc.
Printer and binder: Thomson-Shore, Inc.

Library of Congress Cataloging-in-Publication Data

James, Henry, 1843–1916.
    The correspondence of Henry James and Henry Adams, 1877–1914 /
edited with an introduction by George Monteiro.
        p.    cm.
    Includes bibliographical references and index.
    ISBN 0-8071-1729-3
    1. James, Henry, 1843–1916—Correspondence.   2. Adams, Henry,
1838–1918—Correspondence.   3. Authors, American—19th century—
Correspondence.   4. Authors, American—20th century—
Correspondence.   5. Historians—United States—Correspondence.
I. Adams, Henry, 1838–1918.   II. Monteiro, George.   III. Title.
PS2123.A42     1992
813′.4—dc20
[B]                                                                    91-5175
                                                                       CIP

Letters and excerpts of letters written by Henry James in this volume are quoted
by permission of Alexander R. James; the Massachusetts Historical Society, Boston; and the Henry James Collection (#6251), Clifton Waller Barrett Library,
Manuscripts Division, Special Collections Department, University of Virginia
Library. Letters written by Henry Adams are quoted by permission of the Houghton Library, Harvard University.

The paper in this book meets the guidelines for permanence and durability of the
Committee on Production Guidelines for Book Longevity of the Council on
Library Resources. ∞

*To Brenda*

# CONTENTS

# ILLUSTRATIONS

# PREFACE

All intellectual work is the same,—the artist feeds the public on his own
bleeding insides. Kant's *Kritik* is just like a Strauss waltz.
                                        —William James to Henry James
                                                February 15, 1891

T. S. Eliot ended his review of *The Education of Henry Adams* with
remarks on how Henry James and Henry Adams, in some ways so
similar, differed finally. To Eliot there was nothing to "indicate that
Adams's senses either flowered or fruited," whereas in James it was
evident that although he "was not, by Adams's standards, 'educated,'
but particularly limited," there was a great difference: it was "the sen-
suous contributor to the intelligence [in James] that makes the difference." This conclusion refines on Eliot's observation a year earlier
that James had "a mind so fine that no idea could violate it," for he
was "the most intelligent man of his generation."[1]

Even if, in his notion about James's mind and his insistence that
James was "comparatively parvenu," Eliot presents himself as something of an intellectual snob, he was not wrong about James; but he
was wrong about Adams. Eliot was taken in by the personae Adams
created for the purpose of working an idea through his raw material
in *The Education of Henry Adams*. He did not see, as Adams privately
insisted both to Henry James and James's brother William, that the
book mistitled by its publishers as an autobiography was best seen as
a literary experiment in which both the narrator and the subject, the
manikin or figure the narrator speaks about in the third person, are
literary (one can almost say "fictional") inventions.

Eliot did pay both Adams and James a poet's tribute, if not a critic's, by borrowing from their works for his poetry. "The Love Song
of J. Alfred Prufrock" and "Geronion" would not have been
possible, one is tempted to insist, without Adams' *The Education of*

---

1. T. S. Eliot, "A Sceptical Patrician," *Athenaeum*, May 23, 1919, pp. 361–62;
"In Memory," *Little Review*, V (August, 1918), 46.

*Henry Adams, The Life of George Cabot Lodge, Mont-Saint-Michel and Chartres,* on one hand, and James's *The Ambassadors, The Sacred Fount,* and *William Wetmore Story and His Friends,* on the other.

It is no exaggeration to say, besides, that the two Henrys have had an influence on subsequent American writing that could not have been predicted at the time of their deaths, James's in 1916 and Adams' two years later. The influence of the *Education,* almost a secret force, appears unmistakably in the work of writers, besides Eliot, as diverse as Sherwood Anderson, Vachel Lindsay, F. Scott Fitzgerald, Ernest Hemingway, Eugene O'Neill, Nathanael West, Norman Mailer, and Thomas Pynchon. As for James, it is bootless to compile a comprehensive list that would run from Ezra Pound and Wallace Stevens to Robert Lowell among poets, and Ford Madox Ford and Edith Wharton to Philip Roth and Cynthia Ozick among fiction writers.

That Henry James and Henry Adams had their own relationship should come as no surprise. This volume presents their correspondence, or at least those letters that have survived.

Both sides of the Adams-James correspondence are collected here for the first time and placed in chronological sequence. Earlier appearances of letters, indicated in the notes to those letters, have often been marred by misreadings and unmarked omissions. And since such selections have been presented with other letters to different correspondents and subjected to a general chronology, they have often lost their peculiar flavor and sometimes their point. Restoring them to their rightful place as interrelated elements in an active exchange between two engaging correspondents recaptures something of their original flavor and drama. Since each letter has been freshly edited in its entirety from the manuscript original, I have not found it useful to indicate wherein the present texts differ from those of prior publication.

Covering a thirty-eight-year period, these thirty-six letters constitute the known extant letters exchanged by Henry Adams and Henry James (with four of James's letters to Mrs. Henry Adams [Marian "Clover" Hooper Adams]). Clearly there were more letters written than the three dozen that have survived, but it is not known exactly how many. Some of them were destroyed. At the turn of the century James burned most of his accumulated correspondence.

Adams, for his part, destroyed the bulk of his wife's correspondence shortly after her death in 1885. The four James letters to his old friend Clover Adams survived possibly because Theodore F. Dwight, who served Adams as secretary and who assiduously collected autographs and manuscripts on his own, managed to salvage them for his collection, probably without Adams' knowledge.[2] The upshot is that the thirty-six surviving letters break down somewhat unevenly: twenty-five letters from Henry James to Henry Adams, four letters from James to Marian Adams, and seven letters from Adams to James. So far no letters from Marian Adams to James have turned up.

In transcribing these letters for publication I have followed simple editorial practices. Inside addresses and dates have been placed in the upper right-hand corner of each letter. I have reproduced dates as given, italicizing the customary *d* and *st* when underlined but not the rest of the date when a line has been drawn under it. Complimentary closings and signatures have all been italicized as part of the book's design. Spellings, abbreviations, ampersands, and punctuation have been honored, as well as the placement of punctuation marks within parentheses and outside of quotation marks. Interpolations are enclosed within brackets and the *sic* is employed sparingly to indiate an obvious error in orthography. Punctuation of salutations—comma, period, or dash—has been followed.

I acknowledge the kindness of Lyman Butterfield, who years ago told me about the existence of James's letters to Mrs. Adams and made them available to me. Almost all the surviving letters collected here are in either the Houghton Library at Harvard University or the Massachusetts Historical Society in Boston. One is in the Library of Congress. Edited from the original manuscripts, these letters are published with the consent of those libraries and with the permission, in James's case, of Alexander R. James, the executor of the James estate. Excerpts from letters in the Henry James Collection (#6251), Clifton Waller Barrett Library, Manuscripts Division, Special Collections

2. See Stephen T. Riley's headnote to "A Nugget from the Theodore F. Dwight Papers," *M.H.S. Miscellany*, no. 9 (1966), 1–2.

Department, University of Virginia Library, are quoted by permission of Mr. James and the library.

For their help with the letters in the early stages of this book, I wish to thank Sheila Lennon, Alice Hall Petry, and Philip B. Eppard. Brenda Murphy read the final manuscript. I thank her for her valuable suggestions.

# CHRONOLOGY

1838    Henry Brooks Adams, the third son of Charles Francis Adams and Abigail Brooks Adams, is born on February 16 in Boston, Massachusetts.

1843    Henry James, Jr., the second son and second of five children of Henry James and Mary Robertson Walsh James, is born on April 15 in New York City.

1854    HA enters Harvard College, graduating in 1858 as Class Orator.

1855    HJ attends schools in Europe.

1860    HA serves as private secretary to his father, a congressman from Massachusetts. He publishes letters in the Boston *Daily Courier* and the Boston *Daily Advertiser*.

1861    HA begins seven years of service as private secretary to his father, who is minister to Great Britain. He continues to publish letters in the Boston *Daily Advertiser* and begins his letters to the New York *Times*.

1862    HJ attends Harvard Law School briefly.
        HA continues his letters to the New York *Times*.


1864    HJ publishes his first known book review in the October
        *North American Review* and his first known story (anony-
        mously) in the February *Continental Monthly*.


1867    HA publishes three essays—"Captain John Smith," "Brit-
        ish Finance in 1816," and "The Bank of England Restric-
        tion"—in *North American Review*.


1868    HA reviews Sir Charles Lyell's *Principles of Geology* in *North
        American Review*.
        HJ reviews extensively in *Galaxy, North American Review,
        Nation,* and *Atlantic Monthly*.


1870    HA publishes political articles in *North American Review,
        Westminster Review,* and *Nation*. He is appointed assistant
        professor of history at Harvard College and assumes the
        editorship of *North American Review*.


1871    HA (with Charles F. Adams) publishes *Chapters of Erie, and
        Other Essays*.
        HJ serializes his first novel, *Watch and Ward*, in *Atlantic
        Monthly*.


1872    HA marries Marian "Clover" Hooper on June 27. He con-
        tinues to write for *North American Review*.
        HJ publishes reviews, art criticism, travel pieces, a play, and
        a story.

1875    HJ publishes his second novel, *Roderick Hudson,* and a collection of travel pieces, *Transatlantic Sketches,* writes extensively for periodicals, and moves permanently to Europe, first to Paris, briefly, and then to London.
        HA continues to publish in *North American Review.*


1876    HA edits *Essays in Anglo-Saxon Law,* a collection of essays by different hands.


1877    HA resigns his faculty appointment at Harvard College and moves to Washington, D.C. He edits *Documents Relating to New England Federalism, 1800–1815.*
        HJ publishes his third novel, *The American.*


1878    HJ publishes *Daisy Miller: A Study,* a story that gains him international fame, in *Cornhill Magazine.* He also publishes *The Europeans* and a volume of criticism, *French Poets and Novelists.*


1879    HA publishes *The Life of Albert Gallatin* and *The Writings of Albert Gallatin.*
        HJ publishes *An International Episode, The Madonna of the Future, Confidence,* and *Hawthorne,* a critical study.


1880    HJ begins serialization of *The Portrait of a Lady* and publishes *Washington Square.*
        HA publishes anonymously *Democracy: An American Novel,* a book that causes a considerable stir on both sides of the Atlantic.

1881      HJ returns to the United States. He visits Washington, D.C., staying with Henry and Marian Adams until late January, 1882.

1882      HA publishes *John Randolph* in the American Statesmen series.
In *Century Magazine,* HJ publishes "The Point of View," a story that incorporates some of Marian Adams' remarks.

1884      HA publishes *Esther: A Novel* under the pseudonym Frances Snow Compton.
In the New York *Sun,* HJ publishes "Pandora," a story in which Henry and Marian Adams are fictionalized as the Alfred Bonnycastles. "Pandora" is reprinted in *The Author of Beltraffio* (1885).

1885      Marian Adams commits suicide on December 6. Shortly thereafter HA moves into his house at 1603 H Street.
HJ publishes *Stories Revived* in three volumes.

1886      HJ publishes two novels, *The Bostonians* and *The Princess Casamassima.*
HA tours Japan with the artist John La Farge.

1888      HJ publishes *Partial Portraits, The Reverberator,* and *The Aspern Papers.*

1889      HJ publishes *A London Life.*
HA publishes *History of the United States During the First Administration of Thomas Jefferson.*

1890    HJ publishes *The Tragic Muse*.
        HA publishes *History of the United States During the Second Administration of Thomas Jefferson* and *History of the United States During the First Administration of James Madison*.

1891    HJ has his play *The American* produced. HA attends a performance.
        HA publishes *History of the United States During the Second Administration of James Madison* and *Historical Essays*.

1892    HJ's sister Alice, who had lived in London since 1884, dies.
        HJ publishes *The Lesson of the Master*.
        HA travels to Europe, the first in a series of nearly annual trips that lasts until 1914.

1893    HA prints privately *Memoirs of Marau Taaroa, Last Queen of Tahiti*.
        HJ publishes five books, including *The Real Thing and Other Tales*.

1894    HA publishes "The Tendency of History," his presidential address to the American Historical Association, and tours Cuba with Clarence King.
        HJ publishes *Theatricals* and *Theatricals: Second Series*.

1895    HJ's play *Guy Domville* is produced in London. He publishes *Terminations*.

1896    HJ publishes *The Other House*.

1897    HJ publishes *What Maisie Knew* and *The Spoils of Poynton*.

1898    HJ moves into Lamb House in Rye, Sussex. He publishes *In the Cage, The Two Magics,* and "The Turn of the Screw." HA, with Senator Donald Cameron and his wife Elizabeth, leases Surrenden Dering, a large country house in Kent. HJ visits occasionally.

1899    HJ publishes *The Awkward Age*.

1900    HJ publishes *The Soft Side*.

1901    HJ publishes *The Sacred Fount*.

1902    HJ publishes *The Wings of the Dove*.

1903    HJ publishes *The Better Sort, The Ambassadors,* and *William Wetmore Story and His Friends*.

1904    HA privately prints *Mont-Saint-Michel and Chartres*.
        HJ publishes *The Golden Bowl*. He returns to the United States after an absence of twenty years. He stays with HA in Washington.

1907    HJ publishes *The American Scene* and the first volumes in the New York Edition of *The Novels and Tales of Henry James* (1907–1909).
        HA issues about a hundred copies of the privately printed edition of *The Education of Henry Adams*.

1908    HA aids Clara Stone Hay in the preparation of the privately printed edition in three volumes of *Letters of John Hay and Extracts from Diary.*
HJ's play *The High Bid* is produced.

1910    HJ returns to the United States, publishes *The Finer Grain.*
William James dies.
HA publishes and distributes *A Letter to American Teachers of History.*

1911    HA publishes anonymously *The Life of George Cabot Lodge.*
HJ's *The Saloon,* a one-act play based on the ghost story "Owen Wingrave" (1892), is produced.

1912    HA suffers a stroke on April 24.

1913    HJ publishes the first volume of his autobiography, *A Small Boy and Others.*
HA authorizes a trade edition of *Mont-Saint-Michel and Chartres* under the sponsorship of the American Institute of Architects.

1914    HJ publishes the second volume of his autobiography, *Notes of a Son and Brother,* and a volume of criticism, *Notes on Novelists.*

1915    HJ becomes a British citizen.

1916    HJ is awarded the Order of Merit in January. He dies on February 28.

1917    HJ's unfinished third volume of his autobiography, *The Middle Years,* appears posthumously.

1918    HA dies in Washington, D.C., on March 27. *The Education of Henry Adams* is published in a trade edition and is awarded the Pulitzer Prize the next year.

# ABBREVIATIONS

APM     Henry Adams Papers, microfilm copy, Brown University Libraries, Providence, R.I. The original collection is at the Massachusetts Historical Society.

HL     Houghton Library, Harvard University, Cambridge, Mass.

LC     Library of Congress

MHS     Massachusetts Historical Society, Boston

The Correspondence of
Henry James and Henry Adams

# INTRODUCTION

> To live over people's lives is nothing unless we live over their percep-
> tions, live over the growth, the change, the varying intensity of the
> same—since it was *by* these things they themselves lived.
>                         —Henry James
>                         *William Wetmore Story and His Friends* (1903)

> Henry Adams is as conversible as an Adams is permitted by the scheme
> of nature to be.
>                         —Henry James to Robert Louis Stevenson
>                         February 19, 1893

Henry James knew Marian "Clover" Hooper long before he met
Henry Adams. In an 1869 letter from one of Clover's contemporaries
we read: "I went to a delightful little party of Clover Hooper's, where
I conversed for a long time with your friend Mr. Harry James." And
it was little more than a year later, on May 20, 1870, that James was
writing to Grace Norton about having had lunch with Clover
Hooper, Elizabeth Boott, and others. They sat "on a verandah a long
time immensely enjoying the fun. . . . Mesdemoiselles Hooper and
Boott talked of Boston, I thought of Florence," he wrote, paying his
tribute to the absent Grace Norton. "I wanted to go down to you in
the glade," where he had imagined her to be, "and we should play it
was the Villa Landor. Susan would enact Miss Landor. But the genius
of my beloved country—in the person of Miss Hooper—detained
me."[1] Clover Hooper, even after she became Mrs. Adams, would
always exemplify the genius of America to James, and for years, especially when he published stories such as "The Pension Beaurepas,"
"Point of View," and "Pandora," she would serve as something of a
sympathetic critic as well as his patriotic conscience.

Henry Adams he thought might be a different kind of genius. To

---

1. Rose [Hooper] to Eleanor Shattuck [Whiteside], February 21, 1869, Shattuck Collection, MHS; Leon Edel, ed., *Henry James Letters* (Cambridge, Mass.,
1974–84), I, 240.

Grace Norton he wrote on September 26, 1870: "Do you know Henry Adams?—Son of C. F. A. He has just been appointed professor of History in College, and is I believe a youth of genius and enthusiasm—or at least of talent and energy."[2] As a contributor to the *North American Review,* James would also have been interested in the information that Adams had also assumed that journal's editorship.

On June 27, 1872, Henry Adams married Marian Hooper. In the course of a long honeymoon in Europe, their paths crossed with James's in Rome. That he felt closer to Clover than to her husband is evident in the reference he makes to their meeting in a letter to his father on March 28, 1873. "The Clover Adamses have been here for a week, the better for Egypt, but the worse for Naples, which has made them ail a little. I saw them last p.m., and they are better and laden with material treasures, *à la* Harper." In April, still from Rome, James wrote to his brother William:

> In the way of old friends we have been having Henry Adams and his wife, back from Egypt and (last) from Naples, each with what the doctor pronounced the germs of typhus fever. But he dosed them and they mended and asked me to dinner, with Miss Lowe, (beautiful and sad) and came to Mrs. Summer's, where I dined with them again, and shewed me specimens of their (of course) crop of bric-à-brac and Adams's Egyptian photos (by himself—very pretty)—and were very pleasant, friendly and (as to A.) improved. Mrs. Clover has had her wit clipped a little I think—but I suppose has expanded in the "affections."

In turn, after their return to the United States, Henry James, Sr., kept his second son, Henry, informed of the doings of his friends Marian Hooper and Henry Adams. On October 17, 1873, he wrote: "I lunched in the morning with President Charles Eliot. . . . Godkin and Agassiz and Henry Adams made up the remainder of the members. . . . Agassiz was in great force, stomach and brain both; Henry Adams, saturnine and silent. . . . In the evening I dined at the Gurneys' with Mr. and Mrs. Agassiz, Henry Adams and Clover, and Godkin. Henry Adams, Clover and Ellen [Gurney] all asked

---

2. Edel, ed., *Henry James Letters,* I, 247.

with interest after you, and all expressed pleasure in your literary activity."[3]

When James left Paris in 1876 to make his home permanently in London, he carried letters of introduction to some of Adams' friends, including Sir Robert Cunliffe and Lord Monckton Milnes. "Henry Adams, in the matter of letters," James wrote to his mother, "has come up to time very handsomely and placed me under great obligation to him. Never criticize his 'manners' again."[4] But it was not until Clover and Henry Adams began their periodic traveling abroad that James, in London, got to know them particularly well outside of their Cambridge milieu. In the latter years of that decade, in fact, the two Henrys began to see a good deal of each other on the frequent visits of the Adamses to London.

Clover Adams' letters to her father in the 1870s and 1880s often provide information about James. On June 15, 1879, when the Adamses were living at 17 Half Moon Street, London, she informed him that "Mr. James [lives] in the next street." James visited his American friends often. Sometimes, she complained mildly, he "came in to dine on his own suggestion, and sat chatting till late." While Mrs. Adams was herself being chatty about James, her husband saw things differently. While she was talking about James's coming to tea, Adams was telling his friends, by turns, that James, "in very good condition," was "the most of a society man" he knew and that "Henry James haunts the street gloomily." James, for his part, summed up the young couple. To Elizabeth Boott on June 28, 1879, he wrote: "The Henry Adamses are here—very pleasant, friendly, conversational, critical, ironical. They are to be here all summer and to go in the autumn to Spain; then to return here for the winter. Clover chatters rather less, and has more repose, but she is very nice, and I sat up with them till one o'clock this morning abusing the Britons." To another correspondent he confided, "Adams is very sensible, though a trifle dry," while Clover seems "toned down and bedimmed from her ancient brilliance."[5]

3. *Ibid.*, 360, 368; quoted in Ralph Barton Perry, *The Thought and Character of William James* (Boston, 1935), I, 109.

4. Edel, ed., *Henry James Letters*, II, 92.

5. Ward Thoron, ed., *The Letters of Mrs. Henry Adams, 1865–1883* (Boston, 1936), 140, 155; J. C. Levenson *et al.*, eds., *The Letters of Henry Adams* (Cambridge,

On July 6, 1879, James spent the afternoon with Henry and Clover. To his mother James wrote on the same day: "I went this afternoon with the Henry Adamses to Lady Lindsay's Sunday reception at the Grosvenor Gallery—to which I had asked Lady L. to send them a card. They seemed to enjoy it greatly . . . and they appear indeed to be launched very happily in London life. They are extremely friendly, pleasant and colloquial, and it is agreeable to have in London a couple of good American *confidents*." From Paris in mid-September, 1879, Clover mentioned that Henry James had joined her and her husband for dinner. Still in Paris on her thirty-sixth birthday, she informed her father: "Mr. and Mrs. Jack Gardner, Mr. James, and we to dine in an open-air restaurant and then to the *cirque,* where Mademoiselle Jutan, an angelic blonde, filled our hearts with wonder and joy; then ices on the Boulevard in front of a café, and home at midnight." The three of them were clearly pleased at being on holiday. Their routine went something like this, as she described matters to her father: "Mr. James comes in at about six-thirty and towards seven we go off to dine, and three times a week to the theatre afterwards." A few months later, on January 25, 1880, Clover again complained mildly to her father. "Mr. James . . . comes in every day at dusk & sits chattering by our fire but is a frivolous being dining out nightly. Tomorrow being an off night he has invited himself to dine with us." On February 22, 1880, Adams informed Henry Cabot Lodge: "It is Sunday afternoon. Harry James is standing on the hearth-rug, with his hands under his coat-tails talking with my wife exactly as though we were in Marlborough Street. I am going out in five minutes to make some calls on perfectly uninteresting people." The same day Clover wrote to her father: "People have a bad habit of staying on till midnight which becomes over much—& I think how you would wriggle & sigh. Harry James who comes in of his own accord often is ruthless in that respect. After this I am going to stipulate that I may go at 10½ at latest." Still, in March, when she had a small dinner for "Mr & Mrs Matthew Arnold," the other guests were "Mr James & two or three more." And that summer James continued

---

Mass., 1982–88), II, 366, 368; Edel, ed., *Henry James Letters,* II, 246; and quoted in Arline Boucher Tehan, *Henry Adams in Love: The Pursuit of Elizabeth Sherman Cameron* (New York, 1983), 46.

to be a frequent guest. On July 25, for example, Clover reported to her father: "H. James to dine—very used up with four days of neuralgia in bed—but cheered up with a good dinner"; and on August 29 she informed him that "H. James & Mr. F. Parkman came in that eve$^g$." James, for his part, had become rather attached to Henry and Clover. "I have seen no one here, to speak of," he wrote home, "but the Henry Adamses, who are here for three weeks on their way to Spain, and with whom I fraternize freely. I have become very fond of them—they are very excellent people." The fact of the matter was that he was seeing the Adamses "frequently—almost daily." He wrote, "Henry is very sensible, though a trifle dry, and Clover has a touch of genius (I mean as compared with the usual British Female)."[6]

In December, 1879, appeared the London edition of James's *Hawthorne,* followed in January, 1880, by the American edition. The little book caused a furor in America. James came in for a good deal of harsh criticism. He took his complaints to his friends the Adamses. Clover reported to her father on April 4, 1880: "It is high time Harry James was ordered home by his family. He is too good a fellow to be spoiled by injudicious old ladies in London, & in the long run they would like him all the better for knowing & loving his own country. He had better go to Cheyenne & run a hog ranch. The savage notices of his Hawthorne in American papers all of which he brings me to read, are silly & overshoot the mark in their bitterness but for all that he had better not hang round Europe much longer if he wants to make a lasting literary reputation."[7] Obviously Adams agreed with his wife. Again to Lodge on May 13, 1880, Adams reported: "Harry

6. Edel, ed., *Henry James Letters,* II, 249, 254, 258; Thoron, ed., *Letters of Mrs. Henry Adams,* 178, 182; Marian Adams to Robert William Hooper, January 25, 1880, APM, reel 597; Levenson *et al.,* eds., *Letters of Henry Adams,* II, 393.

7. Marian Adams to Robert William Hooper, April 4, 1880, APM, reel 597. Clover's notion that James might do better by going to Cheyenne to "run a hog ranch" echoes Adams' letter to Sir Robert Cunliffe on July 13, 1879, in which he writes: "As usual, the weather is the chief topic of conversation, always followed by that of American cattle, until my wife says that herds of those beasts pursue her in her dreams and she hears nothing but their mournful bellowing. I think Henry James is regarded as one of them, for—again according to my wife's experience—he is always brought forward as a topic of conversation with these" (Levenson *et al.,* eds., *Letters of Henry Adams,* II, 366).

5

James is expected from Italy at about the same time [as James Russell Lowell]. He gave us his newspaper criticisms to read, but as I've not read his books I couldn't judge of their justice. These little fits of temper soon blow over, however, and if he is good-natured about it he will get straight again soon." When in late September, 1880, the Adamses were about to leave for America, James wrote to Grace Norton:

> I go in an hour to bid farewell to my friends the Henry Adamses, who after a year of London life are returning to their beloved Washington. One sees so many "cultivated Americans" who prefer living abroad that it is a great refreshment to encounter two specimens of this class who find the charms of their native land so much greater than those of Europe. In England they appear to have suffered more than enjoyed, and their experience is not unedifying, for they have seen and known a good deal of English life. But they are rather too critical and invidious. I shall miss them much, though— we have had such inveterate discussions and comparing of notes. They have been much liked here. Mrs. Adams, in comparison with the usual British female, is a perfect Voltaire in petticoats.[8]

Clover Adams, who was herself critical of James's increasingly more obvious preference for things English over most things American, found herself defending her countryman and his books against the very charges brought by others that, in different circumstances, she might herself bring against him. "I stoutly defended Henry James and Daisy Miller to stout Mrs. Smith of Chicago, and protested that the latter was charming and that the author adored her," Clover reported to her father on December 5, 1880. Later she added that Anne Palmer of New York, who had known James in London in 1879, "can't forgive Henry James for his *Daisy Miller,* and, when I said he was on his way home, maliciously asked if he was coming for '*raw* material.' " A few months later, on March 6, 1881, Adams told Sir John Clark that "the American public growls a good deal at having its face slapped; even poor Harry James was a victim." But Clover had her own independent readings of James's fiction. When the au-

8. Levenson *et al.,* eds., *Letters of Henry Adams,* II, 400; Edel, ed., *Henry James Letters,* II, 307.

thor sent her a copy of *The Portrait of a Lady,* his most ambitious novel to date, she wrote to her father on December 4, 1881: "It's very nice, and charming things in it, but I'm ageing fast and prefer what Sir Walter called the 'big bow-wow style.' I shall suggest to Mr. James to name his next novel 'Ann Eliza.' It's not that he 'bites off more than he can chaw,' as T. G. Appleton said of Nathan, but he chaws more than he bites off."[9]

In late 1881, after six uninterrupted years of living abroad, James made an extended visit to the United States. In January of 1882, he visited Washington, D.C. He stayed in rooms at 720 Fifteenth Street, near the Metropolitan Club, but visited often with the Adamses, who were now living permanently in Washington. On January 8, 1882, Clover wrote to her father: "Thursday [January 5], Henry James put in an appearance; that young emigrant has much to learn here. He is surprised to find that he can go to the Capitol and listen to debates without taking out a license, as in London. He may in time get into the 'swim' here, but I doubt it. I think the real, live, vulgar, quick-paced world in America will fret him and that he prefers a quiet corner with a pen where he can create men and women who say neat things and have refined tastes and are not nasal or eccentric." James, for his part, informed Sir John Clark on January 8, 1882:

> I find here our good little friends the Adamses, whose extremely agreeable house may be said to be one of the features of Washington. They receive a great deal and in their native air they bloom, expand, emit a genial fragrance. They don't pretend to conceal (as why should they?) their preference of America to Europe, and they rather rub it into me, as they think it a wholesome discipline for my demoralized spirit. One excellent reason for their liking Washington better than London is that they are, vulgarly speaking, "someone" here, and that they are nothing in your complicated Kingdom.

To E. L. Godkin on January 15, 1882, he was impressed that "the Adamses are always the centre of a distinguished circle," and on January 23, 1882, he wrote again to Sir John Clark.

9. Levenson *et al.,* eds., *Letters of Henry Adams,* II, 421; Thoron, ed., *Letters of Mrs. Henry Adams,* 241, 294, 306.

I see of course a good deal of our little Adamses to whom I gave your message, which they received with pleasure. They don't know I am writing now or they would greet you both affectionately; but Mrs. Adams mentioned to me that she had written to you three or four months ago. I know it would give her pleasure to hear from you again. To do them justice, you should see them in their native air; they take life more easily. They have indeed here a very pretty life.

James continued on in this amiable fashion, describing Washington.

We have some pretty views here, & as Washington is about in the latitude of Palermo, we have, as you may imagine, a good deal of flowing sunshine. But as yet however, it is rather (as almost everywhere here) the possibilities than the actualities that are striking. Fifty years hence this place will probably be (in addition to being the National Capital of a country of a hundred millions of people) one of the most charming winter centres in the world (the summer of course is absolutely torrid.) But meanwhile there is a good deal to be done. If one had a paternal government, addicted to spending money on embellishments, it might be done in ten years, but the Western Congressmen won't vote for such luxuries while they want their own forests cleared & rivers dyked. It has to come gradually, but all that sort of thing, in America, is coming. Meanwhile, however, the countries are pleasantest where it has already arrived.[10]

As it happened, in January, 1882, Oscar Wilde was also in Washington. He, too, was visiting the city for the first time. Wilde's exploitation of the notoriety he had freshly earned in New York was in sharp contrast to James's keen desire to avoid all publicity. As Clover observed, "The newspapers haven't got scent of Henry James yet; he is sheltered under an alias—the Postmaster General, late acting!"[11]

10. Thoron ed., *Letters of Mrs. Henry Adams,* 320; Edel, ed., *Henry James Letters,* II, 366; James to Edwin L. Godkin, January 15, 1882, E. L. Godkin Papers, HL; James to Sir John Clark, January 23, 1882, Henry James Collection, Clifton Waller Barrett Library, Manuscripts Division, Special Collections Department, University of Virginia Library.
11. Thoron, ed., *Letters of Mrs. Henry Adams,* 327.

Nevertheless, each of these transatlantic literary lions, in his own way, became a central seasonal attraction.

James was received in the best places, according to Clover, as well as the worst; but the propriety of sponsoring Wilde split Washington society.[12] At 1607 H Street, the address of the Adamses, Wilde was from the outset decidedly unwelcome, whereas James was a constant guest. Mrs. Adams explicitly asked "James *not* to bring his friend Oscar Wilde"; as she explained to her father, "I must keep out thieves and noodles or else take down my sign and go West." James himself, calling on Wilde upon his arrival in the city, found him to be nothing short of "an unclean beast."[13] But much of Washington society, if not the Adamses, received Wilde with fascination and pleasure.

In New York the editor of the New York *World,* William Henry Hurlbut, had given Wilde a letter of introduction to Harriet Loring, the daughter of Judge Edward G. Loring. When the Lorings subsequently invited Henry and Clover Adams to meet Wilde, they of course declined. As Mrs. Adams wrote, again to her father: "I tartly remarked 'that fools don't amuse me' when a courteous refusal was unheeded. Henry James went to call on him yesterday and says he is a 'fatuous cad.' "[14]

Washingtonians compared and rated the two lions. In a letter to John Hay, dated February 23, 1882, Harriet Loring proved to be no exception. The surprise, however, comes in the nature of her honest but genial observations:

> The season is over and it has not been a gay one but Lent promises to be a season of Wassail. One prominent feature has been the lions that have roared for us—first we had Mr Henry James jr. He liked Washington much and I liked him. I thought him an excellent young man. Very well meaning but very slow minded. "Laborious" describes him I think, his manners and his conversation alike. He is

---

12. James wrote to Edwin L. Godkin that the Adamses disapproved of the company he kept; "though I notice," he continued, "that they are eagerly anxious to hear what I have seen and heard at places which they decline to frequent" (Leon Edel, *Henry James: The Middle Years, 1882–1895* [Philadelphia, 1962], 30).

13. Thoron, ed., *Letters of Mrs. Henry Adams,* 328; Edel, *Henry James: The Middle Years,* 31.

14. Thoron, ed., *Letters of Mrs. Henry Adams,* 333.

always doing his level best and one can't help approving of him but longing for a little of the divine spark. Then we had Oscar. He brought me a letter from W^m Henry H—and burst upon our view one Sunday—tights—yellow silk handkerchief and all. He is the most gruesome object I ever saw, but he was very amusing. Full of Irish keenness and humor and really interesting, either Mr Hurlbut had warned him we were Philistines or he took our measure but he was very unaffected and never posed at all. My father and Mr Bayard thought him very agreeable.

When James was invited to dine with James G. Blaine, Mrs. Adams predictably disapproved. She wrote portentously to her father: "Henry James passed Sunday evening at Robeson's, and dines tomorrow with Blaine. 'And a certain man came down to? from? Jerusalem and fell among thieves . . . and they sprang up and choked him.' " [15]

To Mrs. Isabella Stewart Gardner, James reported at some length in a letter dated January 23, 1882.

I have been here nearly three weeks and I ought to have a good many impressions. I have indeed a certain number, but when I write to you these generalities somehow grow vague and pointless. Everything sifts itself down to *one* impression—which I leave to your delicate imagination. I shall not betray it if I can help it—but perhaps I shan't be able to help it.—Washington is on the whole as pleasant as you told me I should find it—or at least that you had found it. I try to find everything that you do, as that is a step toward being near you. I went last night to the Loring's where you told me you had flung down your *sortie de bal* in the dusky entry, where it looked like a bunch of hyacinths,—and found there the repulsive and fatuous Oscar Wilde, whom, I am happy to say, no one was looking at. —Washington is really very good; too much of a village materially, but socially and conversationally bigger and more varied, I think, than anything we have. I shouldn't care to live here—it is too rustic and familiar; but I should certainly come here for a part of every winter if I lived in the United States. I have seen a good many people, dined out more or less, and tried to make myself agreeable.

15. Quoted in George Monteiro, "A Contemporary View of Henry James and Oscar Wilde, 1882," *American Literature*, XXXV (1964), 530; Thoron, ed., *Letters of Mrs. Henry Adams*, 329.

The Adamses tell me I succeed—that I am better than I was in London. I don't know whether you would think that. I have not fallen in love nor contracted an eternal friendship, though the women, as a general thing, are pleasing. . . . There are . . . some charming girls—not rosebuds, e.g. Miss Bayard and Miss Frelinghuysen, who are happy specimens of the *finished* American girl—the American Girl who has profited by the sort of social education that Washington gives. Plenty of men, of course, more than elsewhere, and a good many energetic types; but few "accomplished gentlemen." I met the President [Chester A. Arthur] the other day (at dinner at Mr. Blaine's) and thought him a good fellow—even attractive. He is a gentleman and evidently has that amiable quality, a desire to please; he also had a well-made coat and well-cut whiskers. But he told me none of the secrets of state and I couldn't judge of him as a ruler of men. He seemed so genial however that I was much disposed to ask him for a foreign mission. Where would you prefer to have me? I wish the States over here would send each other ambassadors—I should like so much to be at the head of a New York legation in Boston—I see a good deal of our excellent Adamses, who have a very pretty little life here. Mrs. A. has perennial afternoon tea—two or three times a day—and frequent dinners at a little round table.

I remain here till the middle of February, and after that I go back to New York for a fortnight.

In the letter to Sir John Clark on the same date James wrote a bit more somberly about President Arthur:

I dined a couple of days ago at Mr. Blaine's, late Secretary of State, to meet the President, whom etiquette permits to dine out but little. He seems a good fellow & a gentleman—he is decidedly *bel homme*—& has the art of pleasing rather more than some of his predecessors. But he is in deep official mourning, his wife is also dead, & the White House is shrouded in gloom. I can see it from these windows as I write—, & there is something dramatic in the vision one can't help having of that solitary individual lifted into a great position by a murder, sitting there in the empty Mansion in which he may hear the hovering of the ghosts of Lincoln & Garfield.

He also said something interesting about Washington's real-life Daisy Millers and Pandoras (one an avatar of the type he had already fictionalized and the other one a second such avatar in the offing). He put his remarks in the context of a heart "half-frozen" in that city in which, he said, "we are having a touch of winter at last in this genial clime."

> I am happy to say that the organ of affection is not otherwise para-
> lyzed—as is fortunate in a country, & above all in a city, in which
> *l'objet aimable* so frequently presents herself. That wonderful prod-
> uct of civilization the American Girl flourishes freely in Washington
> & is on the whole seen here to advantage—as the place affords a
> kind of social education which softens some of her asperities. She
> will not however accompany me back to England in any capacity as
> yet defined.

But the Washington example of the "American Girl," as well as the president, would accompany him to be used in his fiction. Both would emerge fictionalized, along with "the little Adamses, who are (especially Mrs. A.) tremendously political," as the Alfred Bonny-castles in his story "Pandora." [16]

Although James had intended to spend several more weeks in Washington, his stay was cut off abruptly at the end of the month. On January 29, 1882, he was called back to Cambridge because his mother was gravely ill. He returned immediately, but she died while he was en route. Clover wrote to her father on January 31, 1882:

> I've just got a telegram from Mrs. Agassiz in answer to my enquiry
> last night; she says Mrs. James died Sunday night. Henry James
> came here at eleven o'clock Sunday night to tell us he had just re-
> ceived an alarming despatch; he could get no earlier train than yes-
> terday's Limited so he will not reach Cambridge until thirty-six
> hours. It will be a heavy blow to him, the more so perhaps that he
> has been away for six years from her and it's the first time death has
> struck that family. . . . She strongly wished him to live in his own
> country but I doubt if he can; he confesses to being "terribly home-

16. Edel, ed., *Henry James Letters*, II, 372–73, 376; Henry James to Sir John Clark, January 23, 1882, Henry James Collection, University of Virginia Library.

sick for London." He'd better go and lay the ghost, as in the end he must.[17]

James was unable to return to Washington that spring. He remained with his family in Cambridge, largely, until May when he sailed back to England. He wrote a farewell letter to Clover on the eve of his departure. James apparently meant to be complimentary, but Clover was not entirely pleased. On May 14, she wrote to her father: "He [James] wished, he said, his last farewell to be said to me as I seemed to him 'the incarnation of my native land'—a most equivocal compliment coming from him. Am I then vulgar, dreary, and impossible to live with? That's the only obvious interpretation, however self-love might look for a gentler one. Poor America! she must drag on somehow without the sympathy and love of her denationalised children. I fancy she'll weather it!" Shortly after James's arrival in London he ran into Thomas Woolner, the artist and dealer who was a mutual friend. Woolner wrote to Adams on July 31, 1882: "I took my boy Hugh down the river to Greenwich yesterday to divert his mind a little and had dinner at the Trafalgar, where you went with me once, and there we met Henry James who was gentle and pleasant as ever. He seems to me to have unconsciously settled down into being an Englishman, and he only wants an English wife to be one. The truth is one living here long makes so many friends and ties of one kind and another he throws fibres into the soil and becomes a fixture in spirit like a plant in the body."[18]

As soon as James settled back into his London life, he began to write stories that in one way or another reflected his recent American experiences. One of those stories, "The Point of View," appeared in the December, 1882, issue of *Century Magazine*. Clover reacted immediately, writing to her father on November 26, 1882: "By the way, the only letter in Harry James's 'Point of View' in the last *Century* that can hit me is that of Hon. Marcellus Cockrell. Some of the remarks—as that about "Hares and Rabbits Bill and Deceased Wife's Sister'—I plead guilty to, but that it should be spotted as 'one of

17. Thoron, ed., *Letters of Mrs. Henry Adams*, 336.
18. *Ibid.*, 384; Thomas Woolner to Henry Adams, July 31, 1882, Theodore F. Dwight Papers, MHS.

mine' I can't imagine. The whole article seems to me, with one or two exceptions, a dilution of his 'Bundle of Letters' of 1879. The suggestion that 'an aristocracy is bad manners organised' is very good."[19]

Dutifully Clover read everything James wrote, but he was not her favorite writer. "Have read [Francis Marion Crawford's] *Mr. Isaacs* this week and like it," she wrote to her father on January 14, 1883. "It's quite refreshing after the Ann Elizas, Henry James and Howells, etc.—the tiger hunt is very good." In fact, she was a bit disturbed over the controversy that Howells had stirred up when in an article on James in the November, 1882, *Century* he had distinguished between the "modern," more analytical methods of fictional narration as practiced by James (and himself) and the more leisurely, confidential methods of the past, particularly those of Dickens and Thackeray. Adams spoke for Clover as well as for himself when he wrote to John Hay on January 6, 1884: "I admit also to a shudder at the ghastly fate of Harry James and Howells. The mutual admiration business is not booming just now. Between ourselves, there is in it always an air of fatuous self-satisfaction fatal to the most grovelling genius." On the same day, in a letter to her father, Clover put the matter even more directly: "The way in which Howells butters Harry James & Harry James Daudet & Daudet someone else is not pleasant. The mutual admiration game is about played out."[20]

In the spring of 1883 James once again managed to visit Washington. He did not stay with the Adamses but was frequently their dinner guest. It was at one of those dinners, reported Clover Adams, that James first met Elizabeth Cameron (who was to become Henry Adams' great confidante and closest friend) and was "charmed" with her. But otherwise the record is thin for James's Washington visit in 1883. "I spent ten delightful days in New York which decidedly is one of the pleasant cities of the world," he wrote to the publisher Frederick Macmillan on April 19, 1883. "Washington is also charming at present with the temperature of a Northern July, and great banks of pink and white blossom all over the place. It reminds me of

19. Thoron, ed., *Letters of Mrs. Henry Adams*, 403.
20. *Ibid.*, 418; Levenson *et al.*, eds., *Letters of Henry Adams*, II, 527; Marian Adams to Robert William Hooper, January 6, 1884, APM, reel 598.

Rome!" Twenty-five years later, when he was writing the preface for the fourteenth volume of his collected works in the New York Edition, he would recall his Washington lodgings of 1883 as he had remembered them on his more recent visit to Washington in 1905. "The past had been most concretely that, vanished and slightly sordid tenement of the current housing of the muse. I had had 'rooms' in it, and I could remember how the rooms, how the whole place, a nest of rickety tables and chairs, lame and disqualified utensils of every sort, and of smiling, shuffling, procrastinating persons of colour, had exhaled for me, to pungency, the domestic spirit of the 'old South.' I had nursed the unmistakeable scent."[21]

As it turned out, James's visit to the United States in 1882 would not be repeated until 1904. In those twenty years or so, he would continue to see Henry Adams when his friend visited in London or, occasionally, on the Continent. But Clover Adams, after 1883, he would not see again, for Clover died a suicide on December 6, 1885. No longer would James ask mutual friends, such as Edwin L. Godkin, for news of "Mrs. Adam's last," as he did early in the year that she died. The letter of condolence that James must have written to Adams at the time of Clover's death has not survived. But something of James's feelings at the time is revealed in two letters. To Godkin on February 6, 1886, two months after Mrs. Adams' death, he wrote: "I thought of you—and how you would be touched with the sad story, when poor Mrs. Adams found, the other day, the solution of the knottiness of existence. I am more sorry for poor Henry than I can say—too sorry, almost, to think of him." To another correspondent, deploring "the sad rumors of poor Clover's self-destruction," he wrote: "The event had everything that could make it bitter for poor Henry. She succumbed to hereditary melancholia. What an end to that intensely lively Washington salon." It is the suggestion of James's biographer that something of Clover Adams made its appearance in James's fiction within a year after her death. Leon Edel writes: "In a little tale, 'The Modern Warning' . . . Henry James may have incorporated the suicide scene as he re-imagined it—his heroine taking

---

21. Thoron, ed., *Letters of Mrs. Henry Adams*, 443; Edel, ed., *Henry James Letters*, II, 411; Henry James, *The Art of the Novel: Critical Prefaces*, ed. Richard P. Blackmur (New York, 1934), 215.

poison while her husband and brother, to whom she is as attached as Clover was to her father—are out of the house. The lady in the story, however, is not modelled on Clover. She is milder, gentler, less incisive. But the tale itself, with its sharp words between Americans and English—its dialogue between the civilizations of the Old and New World—contains echoes of talk of Henry James with Mrs. Adams." [22]

After his wife's death Adams traveled a good deal by himself and with others, sometimes with John La Farge, at others with Clarence King. With La Farge he went to the South Seas and Japan. Shortly upon his return to America, he moved on to London. He visited James at the time and told him about his South Seas wanderings and unusual experiences, including his pleasant visit with James's friend and fellow-novelist Robert Louis Stevenson. On October 30, 1891, in a letter to Stevenson, James reported what Adams had told him about his visit with the self-exiled novelist.

> I dined last night with Henry Adams, who told me of his visits to you months and months ago. He re-created you, and your wife, for me a little, as living persons, and fanned thereby the flame of my desire not to be forgotten of you and not to appear to forget you. He lately arrived—in Paris—via New Zealand and Marseilles and has just come to London to learn that he can't go to China, as he had planned, through the closure, newly enacted and inexorable, of all but its outermost parts. He now talks of Central Asia, but can't find anyone to go with him—least of all, alas, me. He is about to ship LaFarge home—now in Brittany with his French relations (and whom I have not seen). [23]

By the end of that year Adams was at Tillypronie in Scotland, staying with that great friend to Americans Sir John Clark.

---

22. Edel, ed., *Henry James Letters,* III, 74, 111; quoted in Tehan, *Henry Adams in Love,* 89; Edel, *Henry James: The Middle Years,* 167.

23. Edel, ed., *Henry James Letters,* III, 359–60. One of James's final pieces of dictation, taken down during the last two weeks of December, 1915, refers to Stevenson and, perhaps, Adams: "One of the earliest of the consumers of the great globe in the interest of the attraction exercised by the great R.L.S. [Robert Louis Stevenson] of those days, comes in, afterwards, a visitor at Vailima and [word lost] there and pious antiquities to his domestic annals" (Leon Edel and Lyall H. Powers, eds., *The Complete Notebooks of Henry James* [New York, 1987], 584).

It was at this time that James adapted his 1877 novel, *The American,* for the stage. The play opened in Southport in the provinces on January 3, 1891, where it did well, and later moved to London where it was not a great success. "You can form no idea of how a provincial success is confined to the provinces," he had informed his brother. To Elizabeth Cameron, on November 26, 1891, Adams admitted that he "daren't face Harry James after treating his play as I did." The nature of Adams' treatment, whether he had said something derogatory about the play or had merely neglected to attend either its opening in Southport or one of its London performances, is not known. Less than three weeks later, however, Adams was able to report to John Hay (January 13, 1892) that he had "sat with Harry James an hour or two yesterday afternoon," though he had "found him in double trouble for the death of his friend [Charles Wolcott] Balestier and the steady decline of his sister." Two days later he admitted to Elizabeth Cameron that he had seen, with the exception of one other person, "no one but Harry James." On January 18, 1892, he again evoked James to express to Elizabeth Cameron his own world-weariness: "I feel even deader than I did in the South Seas, but here I feel that all the others are as dead as I. Even Harry James, with whom I lunch Sundays, is only a figure in the same old wallpaper, and really pretends to belong to a world which is as extinct as Queen Elizabeth. I enjoy it. Seriously, I have been amused, and have felt a sense of rest such as I have not known for seven years"—exactly the time that had elapsed since his wife's death. What Adams would have made of James's remarks to Sir John Clark on December 13, 1891, it is futile to speculate. What he says, however, is significant in that James reveals that he has been thinking some about how his situation differs from his friend's.

Many thanks for your sympathetic words about Adams. I like him, but suffer from his monotonous disappointed pessimism. Besides, he is what I should have liked to be—a man of wealth and leisure, able to satisfy all his curiosities, while I am a penniless toiler—so what can *I* do for him? However, when the poor dear is in London I don't fail to do what I can. I don't know where he is now. He kindly forsakes the fleshpots of the Bristol for the very dry *casseroles* of my lofty-lowly garret. I wish you could have had at Tillypronie his and my very old friend (and his late travelling companion) John

La Farge, one of the most extraordinary and agreeable of men, a remarkable combination of France and America, who spent the other day with me in London on his way back to New York, causing me to wonder afresh at his combination of social and artistic endowments and yet how Adams and he could either of them have failed to murder the other in Polynesia. Fortunately each lives to prove the other's self-control.[24]

Every Sunday during his 1892 stay in London, Adams met with James to dine and gossip. The gossip he heard from James on one of those Sundays (and which he repeated to Elizabeth Cameron on January 23, 1892) is probably typical.

Tomorrow, as usual on Sundays, I lunch with Harry James, who is chiefly excited by the marriage of his friend Rudyard Kipling with the sister of another friend, Balestier, an American who was half publisher, half author, and whose sudden death at Dresden a month ago, was a sad blow to James, who depended on him for all his business arrangements. I imagine Kipling to be rather a Bohemian and wanderer of the second or third social order, but he has behaved well about his young woman and has run in the face of family and friends who think him a kind of Shakspeare, and wanted him to marry the Queen or the Duchess of Westminster. I believe his wife is a perfectly undistinguished American, without beauty or money or special intelligence. They were married very privately and almost secretly last week. James had confided it all to me last Sunday, which is the cause of my happening to know about it. James also confided to me his distress because Sergent, the painter, had quarreled with a farmer down at the place, wherever it is, where the Abbey-Millet-Parsons crowd now pass their winters, and after riding up and down his fields of spring wheat, had been wrought to such frenzy by being called no gentleman, that he went to the farmer's house, called him out, and pounded him; for which our artist-genius in America would certainly get some months of gaol, and may get it even here, which much distresses Henry who has a sympathetic heart. This too was confided to me, and has not yet got into the newspapers. As Sergent seems not to distress himself, I see

24. Levenson et al., eds., Letters of Henry Adams, III, 567, 600, 602, 603; Edel, ed., Henry James Letters, III, 367–68.

no reason why James should do so; but poor James may well be a little off his nerves, for besides Balestier's death, the long, nervous illness of James's sister is drawing slowly to its inevitable close, and James has the load of it to carry, not quite alone, for Catherine Loring is here in charge of the invalid, but still the constant load on one's spirits is considerable. I wish I could help him. His sister now keeps her bed, and is too weak to think of anything but her nerves. I sat two hours with Miss Loring yesterday.

Adams' visit to Alice James was noted by her in a diary entry under the date of January 30, 1892: "Mr. Henry Adams said to K. the other day, in discussing the ignorance of the English doctor with regard to the American invalid—'The English doctor before a New England organization is like a pink faced boy with an apple in his hand.' " Within days of that visit Adams had booked passage for America, and after a "parting dinner with James at a restaurant," he sailed on the *Teutonic*.[25]

When James suffered his great humiliation at the opening performance of his play *Guy Domville* in London in 1895, Adams was in Washington. His friend Charles Milnes Gaskell offered him a report on James's ordeal, with which he juxtaposed news of what had befallen that other literary lion who had shared center stage in the literary and political parlors of Washington in 1882. He wrote on April 8, 1895:

> I am very sorry for Harry James' failure, which I hear he takes to heart. The play was from a literary point of view very clever, but dramatically nil. Oscar Wilde's "cause" has filled the papers. . . . What an astounding mystery that passion is! subsisting on the sympathy of discarded valets and grooms, the lowest class I should fancy the human race can produce. Then the way in which they leave their appalling literature about! Lord Douglas gives his coat with the pockets full of these damning letters to a valet and the only friend of mine who ever fell in a similar way did much the same at a London club.

25. Levenson *et al.*, eds., *Letters of Henry Adams*, III, 604–605; Leon Edel, ed., *The Diary of Alice James* (New York, 1964), 228; Levenson *et al.*, eds., *Letters of Henry Adams*, III, 608.

Adams was back in London in 1896. At the end of May, James joined him and their mutual friend John Hay for dinner, and on Derby Day James and Adams were in attendance at a feast hosted by John Hay. By the following spring, Hay had been appointed ambassador to the Court of St. James's. Adams, along with James, paid Hay the honor of meeting his ship at Southampton on April 21, 1897. On May 6, 1897, the new ambassador described the event to Henry Cabot Lodge:

> If you had been at Southampton you would not have had the plea-
> sure of seeing Oom Hendrik [Henry Adams] gloating over my suf-
> ferings. He so thoroughly disapproved of the whole proceeding
> that he fled to the inner-most recesses of the ship—some authorities
> say to the coal-bunkers—out of sight and sound of the whole re-
> volving exchange of compliments. Harry James stood by, and heard
> it all, and then asked, in his mild, philosophical way:—"What im-
> pression does it make on your mind to have these insects creeping
> about and saying things to you?"

Ambassador Hay organized a small group trip to Egypt for early 1897, to which group he hoped to add both Henry James and Henry Adams. Adams did accompany John and Clara Hay, but James begged off reluctantly, knowing it was an opportunity forever lost but also knowing that he could not at that time take such a prolonged journey.[26]

Hay remained in London as ambassador until September, 1898, at which time he returned to the United States to assume the office of secretary of state. However, for the summer of 1898, beginning in June, Adams and Senator Cameron and his wife Elizabeth leased Sur-renden Dering, a large country house in Kent. "The Dering family seat, complete with ancestral portraits and surrounding park," note the editors of Adams' letters, "served as a kind of American hotel for passing statesmen, frequented most particularly by the Hays." James, too, availed himself of these rare opportunities to see his two friends together and on at least two occasions he made his way from Rye to

26. Charles Milnes Gaskell to Henry Adams, April 7, 1895, Adams Papers, MHS; George Monteiro, *Henry James and John Hay: The Record of a Friendship* (Prov-idence, R.I., 1965), 45.

Surrenden Dering, a journey of less than twenty miles. To a friend James wrote, "I have had Henry Adams spending the summer not very far off—in the wonderful old country house of Surrenden Dering, which he has been occupying in the delightful way made possible by the possession of Shekels, in conjunction with the Don Camerons." James, the consummate observer, gleaned a great deal from his two brief stays at Surrenden Dering. Here is how his biographer characterizes James's experience.

He found the summer establishment interesting in many ways, for, as Adams's biographer remarks, "behind the feudal scale of hospitality" there went on the work of diplomacy "as the secretaries hurried back and forth to London." Perhaps even more than in the echoes of Washington within the greenery of Kent, James was interested in the human relations in this large house on the vast estate. He had been fascinated for some time by the way in which Adams had become a part of Elizabeth Cameron's large entourage. "Everyone is doing—to my vision—all over the place—such extraordinary things that one's faculty of wonder and envy begins at last rather to cease to vibrate," he wrote to a friend in Boston. There were signs that his faculty of wonder (like Maisie's [of his novel *What Maisie Knew*]) and his novelist's curiosity were vibrating as strongly as those of his narrator in *The Sacred Fount,* whom he would place two years later on as peopled an estate as Surrenden Dering. Concerning Adams and Mrs. Cameron James remarked that he "envied him as much as was permitted by my feeling that the affair was only what I should *once* have found maddeningly romantic." He had met Mrs. Cameron on other occasions; she was, he found, "hard"—considering her "prettiness, grace and cleverness." The word "clever" in James's lexicon was not always a compliment. Mrs. Cameron was indeed a skilful managerial woman— a Mrs. Touchett or a Mrs. Gereth. Adams's niece, Abigail, has testified that at the manor house that summer Mrs. Cameron "was not only the hostess for this big and complicated caravanserai, but she ran it as well, and I doubt if many details escaped her eagle eye." She was "the most socially competent person that I have ever met," the niece, writing in her old age, remembered—a woman who could "tackle any situation and appear to enjoy it." In his notebooks James wrote that he was "someone haunted with the *American* family, represented to me by Mrs. Cameron," but set this aside as demanding "a large, comprehensive picture." He did not elaborate. The allusion would seem to have been to Mrs. Cameron's ability to be a senator's wife, keep tight control of his busy home and his social life in Washington, and at the same time be available as a social resource and comfort to the widowed Adams. James was to say, in a letter to Henrietta Reubell, two or three years later, in the vein of *The Sacred Fount,* that Mrs. Cameron has "sucked the lifeblood of poor Henry Adams and made him more 'snappish' than nature intended." He added that "it's one of the longest and oddest American *liaisons* I've ever known. Women have been hanged for less— and yet men have been too, I judge, rewarded with more."[27]

In subsequent years, whenever Adams was away from London, either back home in Washington or somewhere on the Continent, mutual friends kept him informed of James's goings and doings. Charles Milnes Gaskell, for instance, told him on April 8, 1899, about the "bad fire in his country cottage" that James had suffered. But after 1898 there was little direct commerce between them for several years. For James the novelist it was a particularly fruitful time, and Adams kept up with his friend through his books. To Elizabeth Cameron he wrote on May 6, 1901, that unlike John Hay, he had not been upset by James's most recent novel, *The Sacred Fount.* Adams recognized that there was "insanity" in the book, a trait which he thought he shared with its author. "I think Harry must soon take a vacation, with most of the rest of us, in a cheery asylum," wrote Adams, adding, "The mistake is in leaving it." The next year his friend Hay recommended *The Wings of the Dove,* characterizing it as "sinfully good." Three weeks later, as he was about to sail for Europe, Adams explained to Hay that "people are talking of books, *L'Associé,* and I don't know what, that I've not read, and keep, like Harry James's, for the voyage." He was keeping Lucien Muhlfeld's novel and, one presumes, James's *The Wings of the Dove* for shipboard reading. After a long silence, on November 18, 1903, Adams once

27. Levenson *et al.,* eds., *Letters of Henry Adams,* IV, 516; Tehan, *Henry Adams in Love,* 152; Leon Edel, *Henry James: The Treacherous Years, 1895–1901* (Philadelphia, 1969), 233–35. Besides its connection to *The Sacred Fount,* Bernard Richards sees a link between James's experiences at Surrenden Dering in the summer of 1898 and his later novel *The Golden Bowl* (Richards, "Henry James's 'Fawns,' " *Modern Language Studies,* XIII [Fall, 1983], 154–68).

again took up his pen to write to James. The immediate occasion was his having just read James's book *William Wetmore Story and His Friends*. If eight and a half months earlier Adams had complained to Elizabeth Cameron that "the generation of Harry James and John Sargent is already as fossil as the buffalo," and that the middle class of Britain, which the painter and novelist had themselves adopted and continued, each in his own way, to portray, "must be exterminated without remorse," now Adams would insist, consistently, that the American generation to which Story (and Adams and James) belonged had lived lives that were superficial and, at the last, "how thin." [28]

In 1904 James returned to the United States for the first time since 1883. James had rented out his "Rye-house" (his "sanctuary," as Adams called Lamb House) to a young married couple of Adams' acquaintance and set out for his visit. Early in January, 1905 (Adams thought James had "fixed on January 10"), James visited Washington to spend, as he told Sarah Butler Wister on the first of the year, "eight or nine days with Henry Adams." He reported to Mary Cadwalader Jones on January 13, 1905, that he found Adams to be "a philosophic father to us." He described him in a different way to Jessie Allen. On January 16, 1905, he wrote: "I am staying with an old friend who has a charming house—Henry Adams, of ancient Presidential race." But his old friend's house was no longer a center for Washington society, as it had been in the 1880s when Clover Adams was alive. For James it was really little more than a convenient and friendly place to stay while he was wined and dined elsewhere. He wrote to Edith Wharton of

> this so oddly-ambiguous little Washington, which sits here saying, forever, to your private ear, from every door and window, as you pass, "I am nothing, I am nothing, nothing!" and whose charm, interest, amiability, *irresistibility,* you are yet perpetually making calls to commemorate and insist upon. One must hold at one's end of the plank, for heaven only knows where the other rests! But, withal, it's a very pleasant, soft, mild, spacious vacuum—peopled,

28. Charles Milnes Gaskell to Henry Adams, April 8, 1899, Adams Papers, MHS; Levenson *et al.,* eds., *Letters of Henry Adams,* V, 248, 420, 464; John Hay to Henry Adams, October 19, 1920 [*sic*], Adams Papers, MHS.

immediately about me here, by Henry Adams, La Farge and St.-Gaudens, —and then, as to the middle distance by Miss Tuckerman, Mrs. Lodge and Mrs. Kuhn, with the dome of the Capitol, the Corcoran Art Gallery and the presence of Theodore—Theodore I—as indispensable *fond!*" I went to Court the other night, for the Diplomatic Reception, and he did me the honour to put me at his table and almost beside him—whereby I got a rich impression of him and of his being, verily, a wonderful little machine: destined to be overstrained perhaps, but not as yet, truly, betraying the least creak. It functions astoundingly, and is quite exciting to see. But it's really *like* something behind a great plate-glass window "on" Broadway.

Adams had been invited to the diplomatic reception but had not gone. In fact, he went out rarely. He did not accompany James on his visit "in the rain to the Washington Cemetery," where James saw the veiled figure by Saint-Gaudens that Adams had had placed at Clover Adams' grave. "James stood for many minutes bareheaded before the solemn bronze figure that seems to embody, more than any work of modern art, that great calm that is beyond hope or fear," wrote Margaret Chanler, who did accompany James to the Rock Creek Cemetery. "He seemed deeply moved." [29]

Shortly after James had left the city, Adams, in letters to Margaret Chanler and to Mary Cadwalader Jones (dated January 27 and 30, respectively) made two references to James that suggest that he had taken his friend's visit in stride. In the first of these references he seems to conflate the titles of two of James's recent novels. "What did I print my books for, at such vast expense to my vanity? Surely not to read them all myself, when one copy is too much! If I do not go about asking all my friends to take them, is it not because I know by a very long experience that no one, however charming, will read without compulsion? I myself read not—no! not even the Golden Fount or Mount or Count or whatever is longer than half a page. Never should I read my own books! they bore me." We do not know if Adams ever did get around to reading *The Golden Bowl,* which was published in America in November, 1904, but he had already read

29. Edel, ed., *Henry James Letters,* IV, 335, 337, 338–39, 341, 342; Mrs. Winthrop Chanler, *Roman Spring: Memoirs* (Boston, 1934), 302.

*The Sacred Fount.* Still, Adams was able to make his point about his readers, or rather his nonreaders. The second reference constituted a complaint in which Adams' tone is difficult to pin down. "Jacobus Magnus of course left no address. I bundle everything to his brother William at Cambridge."[30]

As luck would have it, it was while James was in the United States that he and Adams were elected (in the second round) on January 15, 1905, to the newly created American Academy of Arts and Letters. Neither one of them took the honor entirely seriously. James joked about the uniforms that they might be asked to wear, especially since Theodore Rex (Roosevelt) was also a member. And Adams, faced with the possibility that Joseph Jefferson, the comic actor, might be elected next, wrote to John Hay on May 8, 1905: "[If] Joe Jefferson can be a member, I insist on having some pretty actresses to balance him. I won't stand nonagenarian society. I keep a lot too much in my own skin. I nominate herewith Ethel Barrymore . . . my cousin Maude, Maxine Elliot, Elsie Dewolfe[,] Mrs. James Brown Potter[,] Nan Patterson to begin with, and of course shall insist on Bessie Marbury, Edith Wharton and Mrs. Winty to make us respectable."[31]

On November 7, 1905, to Anna Cabot Mills Lodge, Adams surprisingly introduced James's name in a discussion of the American woman.

> The revolt of the American woman has taken portentous proportions. . . . If you want to know the American, come here [to Paris]! You'll never see him at home. There she says she just adores Chicago. And I guess our poor husbands believe it. The French say that there is always a shade of ridicule in the position of husband. I am getting to think there is more than a shade of ridicule in the position of male. The American man is—a—chump! Luckily he will never be clever enough to know it, and the American woman seems likely to be clever enough to hide it from him. As long as he can run a machine he will never concern himself about a human, and naturally he takes to the easier job. Ah! if Harry James only understood!

If Adams still had doubts in 1905 as to whether James showed any real understanding of the American man, twenty years earlier in a

---

30. Levenson *et al.*, eds., *Letters of Henry Adams,* V, 630, 631.
31. *Ibid.,* 656–57.

letter to John Hay (September 24, 1883) Adams had impugned
James's knowledge of women. Praising its author, he would not hes-
itate to put the novel *The Bread-Winners* "quite at the head of our
Howell's-and-Jame's [*sic*] epoch for certain technical qualities, such as
skill in construction, vivacity in narration, and breadth of *motif*. It has
also one curious and surprising quality, least to be expected from an
unknown western writer. Howells cannot deal with gentlemen or ladies; he always slips up. James knows almost nothing of women but
the mere outside; he never had a wife. This new writer not only
knows women, but knows *ladies;* the rarest of literary gifts."[32]

In the next few years, after 1905, Adams and James saw each
other occasionally, usually in London or Paris. In May, 1907, James
visited Adams in Paris. It was around this time that Adams, because
William James had requested a copy, finally sent his wife's old Cambridge friend the *Education*. After explaining his motivation and in-
tentions to William, he took leave of the book (December 9, 1907).
"The devil take it! I feel that Sargent squirms in the portrait. I am not
there. You, at least, and your brother Harry, have been our credit and
pride. We can rest in that." A little over two months later, on February 17, 1908, Adams began another letter to William James: "As a wit
and humorist I have always said that you were far and away the superior to your brother Henry, and that you could have cut him quite
out, if you had turned your fun that way. Your letter is proof of it."
James had written a critique of the *Education* in which he had said,
among other things, "Parts of it I find obscure, but parts of it (as
the curate at the Bishop's table said of the egg) are excellent, superla-
tively so."[33]

All the while Adams continued to read Henry James's latest
books. His reading included, as one might have expected, *The American Scene,* James's book on his American travels during 1904–1905.
In a letter to Blanche Tams, on April 3, 1908, Adams referred to what
in that book James had said about Washington. The city "is already
at its best," he said, "all the streets and woods are yellow, and, at the
end of the long bowered vistas, the bronze generals, whom Henry

32. *Ibid.,* 721, II, 512–13.
33. *Ibid.,* VI, 92, 119; Elizabeth Hardwick, ed., *Selected Letters of William James*
(New York, 1961), 242.

James so justly wishes were fauns and naiads, cut the distance with scissors. It is inconceivable what a bore the American statesman is! Even in death he bores." [34]

When Adams returned to Paris in early May, 1908, James was already there. To Charles Milnes Gaskell on May 6, 1908, Adams wrote: "As I arrived only three days ago, on Sunday, I have little or nothing to tell you about art, or literature or drama. I find Henry James here, to remind me that people as old as I still seem to exist, but he knows nothing of news. . . . Positively, at times I feel altogether detached from space and time. If I were not so irritable, I should float like a death's-head moth." On the same day, Adams finally sent James his copy of the *Education*. Two days later Adams joined James (along with William Dean Howells and his daughter Mildred) in a private luncheon given by the American ambassador, Henry White. On May 14, 1908, to Elizabeth Cameron, he mentioned James twice. "I tried an hour or two of Jeanne Granier at the Vaudeville the other evening, but found it enough, without the Third Act," he wrote. "Edith Wharton and Henry James had the same experience with La Vallieré at the *Variétés*." He also told her that James had been painted by Jacques Emile Blanche. "Who is Blanche?" he asked. "He was at the Embassy dining last night, but I know his work no better." On May 20, 1908, to Mabel Hooper La Farge Adams wrote that Edith Wharton had taken him the day before "to see a portrait of Henry James in Blanche's studio." Four days later he told Elizabeth Cameron disapprovingly that "Blanche, the young painter," had "perpetrated a rather brutal, Sargenty portrait of Henry James." (In fact, he wrote to George Cabot Lodge on April 22, 1909, that "Blanche's portrait" portrayed "Henry James as Lord Chancellor.") But by then Europe was "duller than boarding school" to Adams, who complained that Henry James, with "no reserves to open before my glad eyes, . . . seemed even more isolated than I." [35]

In 1910 Henry James suffered a nervous breakdown. When Adams learned about James's collapse, he wrote to William James, who was then in Rye (or so Adams thought) to care for his brother.

34. Levenson *et al.*, eds., *Letters of Henry Adams*, VI, 130.
35. *Ibid.*, 135, 141, 144, 146, 245; Harold Dean Cater, ed., *Henry Adams and His Friends* (Boston, 1947), 625.

In a letter dated May 8, 1910, Adams wrote: "From Mrs. Wharton I learn that your brother is ill, and that he is not disposed to correspondence. She tells me that you are with him, which is an extra reason for my asking both your newses. If you are not overwhelmed by the social absorptions of Rye, and can overcome your anguish at the departure of our old friend and companion the King [Edward VII had died on May 6, 1910], I wonder whether you could scratch a line to tell me how your brother is doing, and how you are helping him to do." William, who was himself suffering from a serious heart condition, was no longer in Rye, having left on May 5, 1910, for treatment in Germany. Adams later saw him in Paris. "William James came through with a heart or something for Nauheim," Adams wrote to Anna Cabot Mills Lodge on May 17, 1910. "His brother Henry bobs up and down with melancholia. I fear that both of them take themselves seriously and have an idea that they are somebodies which accounts for it." On August 26, 1910, William James died. On September 22, 1910, Adams wrote to Charles Milnes Gaskell: "As for America, it is, long since, intellectually paralysed. Poor William James set up for our last thinker, and I never could master what he thought. His brother Henry is still in America, and I fear is in a poor way, which his brother's death did not help." Two weeks later, in a letter to James Ford Rhodes, Adams wrote playfully: "I am heartily glad to hear that you are doing well, and recovering your normal strength. Boston needs you. If you have lost William James, I hope you will at least profit by Henry's presence. He is a post-prandial whale. He rolls over the conversational ocean like poor old John Fiske." Yet just a few weeks later Adams admitted that according to Edith Wharton, James was "in a very bad way." Adams wrote as much to Bernhard Berenson on November 30, 1910. In a letter to Mabel Hooper La Farge eight days later, he apparently was no longer thinking about James's health but commenting on his most recent book, along with Edith Wharton's work: "[Her] stories show the strain she is under, and Henry James's volume [*The Finer Grain*] is not quite his best." On December 14 he returned to the matter of James's health, writing to his friend Gaskell: "My friends die daily. John LaFarge dropped out, the other day. William James preceded him a week or two. Alex Agassiz passed first, in the summer. I am far from easy about Henry James, and as for my other invalids I pass my time in holding their hands." On the last day of the year 1910, a good day for morose thought (though Adams usually needed no such excuse), Adams wrote to Charles Milnes Gaskell: "I've nothing to complain of. Nobody seems to care to read by my light, but by whose light does anybody read? Even Rudyard Kipling's has already died out. Henry James is forgotten. I doubt whether all the Magazines can now rake up a writer who would be sure of sale. I am still surer they could hardly rake up one who would deserve it." [36]

When in mid-January, 1911, Adams arrived in the United States, he found that James was still in America. He was staying in New York at Mary Cadwalader Jones's. "Mrs. Jones, too, and the Brices, offer tea and meals," he wrote to Elizabeth Cameron, "and Roosevelts and Henry James and so on." He expected James to stay with him when he came to Washington as planned on March 15, 1911. To Edith Wharton, on February 9, 1911, James himself wrote that New York had given him the "tenderest nursing" care and that he might now be ready (he was still under treatment for his nervous collapse) to "snatch a 'bite' of Washington (Washington pie, as we used to say), to which latter the dear H. Whites" had "most kindly challenged" him. To Mary Cadwalader Jones, on March 18, 1911, Adams wrote: "I am glad to hear that you have recovered Henry James and that he seems to have recovered himself." Later in the same year (October 5, 1911), writing once again to Mary Cadwalader Jones, Adams complained that he no longer heard news about anyone. "I have no one to tell me what to say about matters here," he wrote. "Truly I wonder what my contemporaries do for an occupation. What is Henry James doing? I suppose he is nursing himself as I do. Why don't they tell me so? They must know it would be a great comfort to me to know that they were suffering." In the same letter, with James still on his mind, he wrote: "Presently I suppose some lady will pass by, and will take me by the ear, and lead me home [he was in Paris]. I feel like my poor father after he lost his mind, like Elisabeth, and could not tell where he was. I do not know how to get home, for my cook is better here,

36. Levenson *et al.*, eds., *Letters of Henry Adams*, VI, 335, 336–37, 371, 375, 387, 390, 393–94, 398.

only I've no means of warming my rooms. Under such circumstances, what would Harry James do? Obviously, get a social secretary."[37]

In April, 1912, Adams suffered a stroke. When his family effectively discouraged Elizabeth Cameron from going to him, James wrote to her understandingly: "I can't help feeling with a pang or at least a groan that your going over to the dire American midsummer may be involved. To speak crudely and familiarly they clearly—by all their gestures—'don't want you' (and by they I mean simply They). So that if your dear Henry should have difficulties of communication, expression or even perception, they will overflow with superiority." The next year, writing again from Paris on June 29, 1913, Adams wrote somewhat bemusedly to Elizabeth Cameron:

> From home I hear little or nothing, for my brother Brooks is sailing for England, and I fear that Nanny is not. Bessy is in the struggle of moving to Paris Plage. Mrs Wharton goes to England tomorrow. None of them talk of Boston. None of them seems to think of anything but passing the summer.
>
> It is a wierd and unearthly effect to us who have things on our minds. To me it is at times incredible. At about three in the morning I wobble all over the supposed universe. A little indigestion starts whole flocks of strange images, and then I wonder what Henry James is thinking about, as he is my last standard of comparison.

James continued to be Adams' standard of comparison. When Adams got on to the topic of how readers neglected him, he wrote: "So obsolete am I that no one ever heard of me. People send me press-notices of Chartres, and not one has yet been aware that I ever wrote anything else. To be sure, poor Harry James is worse off, and is treated with more disrespect, but then I have the architects behind me. Poor Henry is quite alone. No one has ever heard of him."[38]

In August, 1914, war broke out. James was greatly distressed over what he called "the funeral speech of our murdered civilization." On August 21, 1914, he revealed his anguish to Mrs. John La Farge.

37. Ibid., 418, 427, 475; Edel, ed., Henry James Letters, IV, 574.
38. Tehan, Henry Adams in Love, 246; Levenson et al., eds., Letters of Henry Adams, VI, 604–605, 642.

I write you under the black cloud of portentous events on this side of the world, horrible, unspeakable, iniquitous things—I mean horrors of war criminally, infamously precipitated. What point of danger the situation may have reached this soft mid-summer Sunday night we shan't know till the morning; but the air is full of the wars, and rumors, and I brace myself with the fear of the newspaper. These are monstrous miseries for *us* of our generation and age, to live on into; but we wouldn't not have lived—and yet this is what we get by it. I try to think it will be *interesting*—but have only got so far as to feel it's sickening.

Learning that Adams was staying that August with Elizabeth Cameron at Stepleton, James motored over to visit him. Aileen Tone later described "the encounter of the two Henrys, how they threw their arms around each other as if bridging a great chasm." To Edith Wharton, James reported on a later visit with his old friend in October.

Yesterday I saw Henry Adams and his two young nieces, the natural and the artificial; in fact I dined with them last night at their hotel, to which they had come from their stay of several weeks at the Cameron-Lindsay place in Dorsetshire—in order to sail for home to-day in some White Star thing of which I forget the name. Henry, alas, struck me as more changed and gone than he had been reported, though still with certain flickers and *gestes* of participation, and a surviving capacity to be very well taken care of; but his way of life, in such a condition, I mean his world-wandering, is all incomprehensible to me—it is so quite other than any I should select in his state.

As it turned out, this was the last time they would see each other. Neither of them would last out the war.[39]

On December 2, 1915, Henry James suffered a stroke. Elizabeth Cameron kept Adams informed of James's condition. "It is slight so far and it affects only his left side," she wrote encouragingly at the outset. But his condition would quickly deteriorate, though he would linger for nearly three months. On December 28, 1915,

---

39. Tehan, *Henry Adams in Love*, 254; John La Farge, S.J., "Henry James's Letters to the LaFarges," *New England Quarterly*, XXII (1949), 192; Lyall H. Powers, ed., *Henry James and Edith Wharton: Letters, 1900–1915* (New York, 1990), 312–13.

Adams, back in Washington, wrote to Elizabeth: "What you tell me of Harry James is suggestive. I am heaps older than Harry, and had my stroke near four years ago, but it brings one blessing—it wipes out the future, and leaves precious little of the present." What Elizabeth had told him on December 24, 1915, was that James was "still living, " though his mind was "more clouded." Adams reacted further to Elizabeth's sickroom bulletins in a letter on January 10, 1916: "My heart is sore for mine own people. War is a light affliction. Here am I in full peace who have lost not only my brother, but Nanny Lodge, and now you tell me of Harry James. Only a few old imbeciles are left." On February 6, 1916, again to Elizabeth, he mentioned that all his "contemporaries have got paralysis, like Harry James . . . , and I got paralysis four years ago by way of being ahead of the procession." The day after James's death on February 28, 1916, Adams wrote to Elizabeth:

> Today, the death of Harry James makes me feel the need of a let-up; I must speak to some one, and here I have no one Jamesian to talk to, except Wendell Holmes, and I never see him; for he is like me in avoiding contemporaries. Harry's death hits me harder than any stroke since my brother Charles' death a year ago. Not only was he a friend of mine for more than forty years, but he also belonged to the circle of my wife's set long before I knew him or her, and you know how I have clung to all that belonged to my wife. I have been living all day in the seventies.

It is significant that James's death brought Adams to do something he had rarely done after 1885: he mentioned Clover.[40]

Two and a half weeks later on March 18, 1916, Adams wrote to Charles Milnes Gaskell, one of the first of his English friends and to whom Adams had introduced James in 1877: "All this long winter I've sat, looking into the fire, thinking about you and our friends abroad, but afraid to say a word for fear of more bad news. I was hit badly by Harry James's collapse, and yet Harry went to live in England only long after I left it. He was a very old friend—but not as old as you."[41] Adams died two years later, on March 27, 1918.

40. Tehan, *Henry Adams in Love*, 257; Levenson *et al.*, eds., *Letters of Henry Adams*, VI, 712, 715, 716n, 721, 724.
41. Levenson *et al.*, eds., *Letters of Henry Adams*, VI, 726.

## 1  JAMES TO ADAMS

3 Bolton St.
Piccadilly
[London]
Jan. 13*th* [1877]

My dear Adams—

You have certainly come up to time with your introductions, beyond my expectations or my merits. I don't know which to rate more highly, the benevolence of your letters, or their versatile cleverness. I feel as if my sails were filled by celestial zephyrs, & I should be floated directly to the islands of the Blest. Your friends are evidently charming people, from the way you write to them. After I have had the pleasure of making their acquaintance I shall make a point of giving you news of them. This, meanwhile, is only to acknowledge & thank you for your packet, which arrived this a.m.[1] Your picture of Boston with its gorgeous Turners and its frescoed churches, is really glowing, & I feel like hurrying home, to become the Vasari of such a Florence, where indeed I advise you to remain & become the Machiavelli.[2] I can think of no fair old Tuscan who deserves that your wife should take her for a precedent.

*Very truly & gratefully yours,*
*H. James jr.*

MS  MHS

1. Years later James recalled the autumn of 1876 when he arrived in London. "I first took up my abode in Bolton St. I had very few friends, the season was of the

darkest and wettest, but I was in a state of deep delight. I had complete liberty, and the prospect of profitable work; I used to take long walks in the rain. I took possession of London; I felt it to be the right place. I could get English books: I used to read in the evenings, before an English fire. I can hardly say how it was, but little by little I came to know people, to dine out, etc. I did, I was able to do, nothing at all to bring this state of things about; it came rather of itself. I had very few letters—I was afraid of letters. Three or four from Henry Adams, three or four from Mrs. Wister, of which I only, as I think, presented one (to George Howard)" (Edel and Powers, eds., *Notebooks*, 218).

2. James refers here to the paintings of Joseph Mallord William Turner (1775–1851), the English painter famous for his sunsets and seascapes.

## 2   JAMES TO ADAMS

(Bolton St. W.)
[London]
May 5*th* 77.[1]

My dear Adams.

Of course this letter has been mentally begun several dozen times before this; & equally of course, London being London & the huge high-pressure machine you know, it has never found a moment when it could emerge from my yearning intellect. I wanted to write to you, but I consoled myself for delay with thinking that the longer I waited the more I should have to tell you. I have waited so long now that I am quite embarrassed with confidences, & I have let so many of my impressions grow old that some of them have forgotten that in their innocent youth they were very lively. I have really become something of an old Londoner; I am, for instance, so stupidly, prosaically, insensibly, at home, in this blessed asylum of an Athenaeum Club that I feel as if I were losing half its charm—a charm to be properly enjoyed by a Western barbarian only in a flutter of luxurious appreciation. But the flutter will come back when I am turned forth in the cold world again!—I suppose you have heard from any member of my family whom you may have lately encountered that I am having a "beautiful time" and drinking deep of British hospitality. Such a view of the case is in the main correct; but in writing to my relatives I ransack my memory for every adventure that has befallen me & turn my pockets inside out; so that they receive, & possibly propagate, an exaggerated impression of my social career. I didn't come here on a lark, but to lead my usual quiet workaday life, & I have limited myself to such entertainment as was consistent with this modest programme. But I have little by little seen a good many people—gathered a good many impressions & largely enjoyed things. Brutally speaking, I like London exceedingly. I find it very much the place for me, & when I first came here (for I liked it from the first) I seriously regretted that I had wasted time in not fixing myself here before. That, however, I have ceased to regret; for it is a great advantage to be able to compare London with something that is not London—an advantage to one's self I mean: not always an advantage to London! Your introductions rendered me excellent service & brought about some of the pleasantest episodes of my winter. I am an old friend of the Cunliffes; I have seen, for London, a good deal of them.[2] A capital couple they are, & their friendliness & attentiveness have been more than fraternal. Cunliffe himself is out of town, on some (by me imperfectly realised) militia duty in the country; but I spent an afternoon with him just before he departed. We went out to Richmond by train one lovely day, & took a long charming walk in the Park; one of those agreeable things one can do so easily & compactly here. The last I saw of Lady C. (whom I find a most sweet, frank, comfortable creature,) was at the private view of the Royal Academy, where I walked about with her & pretended to think some of the dreary daubs worth pointing out to her. You can't, after all, say to an Englishwoman, even if she be as gentle & liberal as Lady Cunliffe, that you think her nation fatally unendowed for the arts, & her Royal Academy the biggest vulgarity of the age. The exhibition this year seems like a collection of colored lithographs from music sheets.[3]—Lord Houghton has been my guide, philosopher & friend—he has breakfasted me, dined me, conversatzioned me, absolutely caressed me.[4] He has been really most kind & paternal, & I have seen, under his wing, a great variety of interesting & remarkable people. He has invited me to an evening party tonight (but you see I prefer to sit here, & scribble to you; it's 1/2 past 11;) & to a 6th or 8th breakfast next week. So you will perceive he has done very handsomely, & I will defend him with my latest breath! Palgrave I have not seen so often; but I have seen (not to say heard!) a good deal of him when we *have* come together.[5] I have been two or three times to see him of an evening & have sat late talking with him *de omnibus rebus*. At first, to speak frankly, I didn't like him; but each time we have met I have thought better of him. He pitches into people too promiscuously; but this, I think, is but a conversational habit begotten of the exuberance of his faculty for talking, & in the long run I suspect he will turn out as kind as he is clever. He *is* a most mighty talker, & a very good one. Woolner & his picturesque, amiable wife I have seen three or four times—the last one on the occasion of his showing me 2 water-colors (a Cotman & a Bonnington) which he was on the point of sending out to you.[6] He wanted to know what I thought of the selection. I approved it highly and thought the Cotman (a seapiece,) superb. There was another C. which I a little preferred (an old Normandy house:) but only for extrinsic reasons—such as your already having a marine Cotman. Woolner's choice is quite the stronger picture. I find W. a very honest, vigorous fellow &, for an Englishman, quite a handsome sculptor.[7]—I said above that I have seen a good many people—which is true with the emendation that I have had very little contact with individuals in the mass. I have formed no "relations" of any consequence, & made no intimacies; what I have done has been simply to get a rough sense of London, to feel that it is a place where almost anything or any one may turn up, & to like it accordingly. I like it so well that I shall certainly if nothing interferes make it my local anchorage for the rest of the time that I remain in Europe; which will more probably be long than short. Heaven knows one is an outsider here: but the outsider that one must be in Europe one is here in the least degree. So at least I feel; and at any rate I have got thus far with London, that I am not afraid of it—not at all. At the same time I don't think I could stomach any long residence here that should not be interspaced with periods (in summer & autumn) of the continent.—There are 20 pages of egotism for you; but I believe that both you & your wife will take it kindly. I have left myself no space for inquiries as to your own present situation; but I am reassured by my impression that this is always intrinsically comfortable. I suppose you are on the point of exchanging Boston for Beverly—bless them both![8] I only wish you a less ferocious May than this, here, which is paying us off for what seemed a very innocent winter. Give

my friendliest remembrances to your wife & believe always very
truly yours

H. James jr.

MS MHS

1. Printed in Edel, ed., *Henry James Letters*, II, 109–12.
2. Sir Robert Alfred Cunliffe (1839–1905) and Eleanor Sophia Egerton Leigh,
his first wife.
3. Not to Lady Cunliffe could James say such things, perhaps, but to an American public he held back nothing. He writes in "The Picture Season in London" in
the August, 1877, *Galaxy*: "That the people he lives among are not artistic, is, for
the contemplative stranger, one of the foremost lessons of English life; and the exhibition of the Academy sets the official seal upon this admonition. What a strange
picture-world it seems; what an extraordinary medley of inharmonious forces!" Of
the Royal Academy "of the present moment," James writes that it "unquestionably
represents a great deal of cleverness and ability; but in the way in which everything
is painted down to the level of a vulgar trivial Philistinism there is something sig-
nally depressing. And this painting down, as I call it, seems to go on without a
struggle, without a protest on the part of the domesticated Muse, with a strange,
smug complacency on the part of the artists. They try of course to gather a little
prettiness as they go, but some of them succeed in a measure which may be appreciated; for the most part I confess they seem to revel in their bondage and to accept
as the standard of perfection one's fitness for being reproduced in the *Graphic*" (John
L. Sweeney, ed., *The Painter's Eye: Notes and Essays on the Pictorial Arts by Henry James*
[Cambridge, Mass., 1956], 148).
4. Richard Monckton Milnes, Baron Houghton (1809–1885), befriended many
Americans, including Henry Adams and John Hay. Adams had given James a letter
of introduction to Lord Houghton (referred to by some as the "bird of paradox").
He was famous for his celebrity breakfasts.
5. Francis Turner Palgrave (1824–1897), art critic, minor poet, and one-time
Professor of Poetry at Oxford, is now chiefly remembered for his anthology *Golden
Treasury of the Best Songs and Lyrical Poems in the English Language* (1861). James was
not much taken with Palgrave. To his brother William he wrote on March 29, 1877:
"Did I tell you that I some time since spent an evening with F. T. Palgrave? Strictly
between ourselves—i.e. as regards H. Adams, and everyone else,—I don't particularly like him: but he is evidently very respectable. He is a tremendous case of culture, and a 'beggar for talk' such as you never faintly dreamed of. But *all* his talk is
kicks and thrusts at every one going, and I suspect that, in the last analysis, 'invidious
mediocrity' would be the scientific appellation of his temper. His absence of the
*simpatico* is only surpassed by that of his wife. (This sounds pretty scornful; and I
hasten to add that I imagine he very much improves on acquaintance. I shall take a
chance to see" (Leon Edel, ed., *Selected Letters of Henry James* [Cambridge, Mass.,
1987], 148). Despite this unpromising start, James and Palgrave did become friends,
a friendship that lasted until the latter's death; see Gwenllian F. Palgrave, *Francis*

*Turner Palgrave: His Journals and Memories of His Life* (London, 1899), 163–64, 218–19, 257–58.

6. Thomas Woolner (1825–1892) was best known as a sculptor, but he also had a small reputation as a Pre-Raphaelite poet. John Sell Cotman (1782–1842) was an English water-colorist and landscape painter. Richard Parkes Bonington (1801–1828) was another English landscape painter and water-colorist. James misspells his name.

7. Woolner's own letter to Adams anticipated James's letter by six days. On April 29, 1877, he had written: "One thing has kept me thinking how to make up the sum you sent in drawings. I had thought of a large powerful Sea Piece by Cotman; but, as you had mentioned De Wint and Copley Fielding, and I had no water colour by either I was wondering what I could do to make any similitude with your idea; happily your friend James called yesterday, and having stated the case to him he judged as I had done myself, and as I should like to have judged in my own case, and he decided for the great Cotman Sea Piece. It costs you £35—completing the £100—you sent" (John F. Cox, ed., "Some Letters of Thomas Woolner to Mr. and Mrs. Henry Adams [I]," *Journal of Pre-Raphaelite Studies,* I [May, 1981], 9).

8. The Adamses spent summers in Beverly Farms, Massachusetts.

## 3   JAMES TO ADAMS

[London]
May 31st [1877]

My dear Adams—

It is time I should write you a line to explain the non arrival of your case of pictures. I was altogether rejoiced to be of any service in forwarding the same & accordingly Woolner made it over to me. On the following day, with his family, he left town "for the North." On the day after he had left town I repaired with the case to the American consul's, & there learnt to my dismay that the necessary affidavit could be made only by the examiner and sender of the contents of the box in *person.* This was an immutable decree: tho' I wrestled with the consul, figuratively, some 1/2 hour to produce a mutation. I then wrote to Woolner telling him the tale, & asking when he should be again in London. Mrs. W. answered me from Edinburgh that her husband would be in town in a few days & would then accompany me to the consul's. He hasn't yet turned up (this was 15 days ago) but he doubtless will, presently, & then we will put the thing thro! Meanwhile I write these few words simply to reassure you (as you probably heard from W. that your drawings were starting,) & not in the least to give you the shadow of an idea that the matter gives me the smallest trouble. (Excuse my 1/2 sheets.) The case is in my safest keeping, & it is a keen satisfaction to take care of it, after all your favors to myself. *Pazienza,* then, for a few days longer. I see (by W.'s invoice) that he has sent you 6 drawings instead of the 3 he had decided upon when I last saw him. I don't know what these are, but doubt not they are handsome.—I don't mean this for a letter; I wrote you one a month ago. Lady Cunliffe told three days since (with an air of extreme delight) that she had just got a very charming letter from Mrs. Adams. I have a plan to go this next week with Cunliffe down to Hatfield for the day. They leave town (the C.'s) presently "for good," & let their London house. I am very sorry—speaking as one who counts upon future winters in London. I am more & more domiciled & contented here. I went yesterday to the ferry on top of a coach, &, in spite of my elevation found it "low."—I have just learned [of] poor Motley's death; which on the whole doesn't surprise me, as he struck me before he left London, as rather a "finished" man.[1] He was, before doing so (leaving London,) very kind to me; & I am particularly sorry for his poor unmarried daughter, having as she does now before her the lot of a parentless spinster in England. But she is an interesting girl & oughtn't to remain a spinster.—I suppose you are facing toward Beverly. Wherefore I envy you, & yet don't. I have just been strolling in Kensington Gdns & sitting a bit in the Park which just now in the freshness of their green are a very pretty Beverly. With very cordial greetings to your wife

*Yours very faithfully*
H. James jr.

MS   MHS

1. John Lothrop Motley (1814–1877), the American diplomat and historian, was best known for *The Rise of the Dutch Republic* (1856). He befriended James on the latter's arrival in London. As James recorded in a notebook, "Poor Motley, who died a few months later, and on whom I had no claim of *any* kind, sent me an invitation to the Athenaeum, which was renewed for several months, and which proved an unspeakable blessing" (Edel and Powers, eds., *Notebooks,* 218).

## 4  JAMES TO ADAMS

[London]
June *5th* [1877]

Dear Adams—

Your case leaves London this p.m. by Starr, & L'pool in the Thursday (June 7th) steamer. Here is the receipt.[1] I wish it *bon voyage* & a prompt delivery. I was with Woolner at the Consul's this a.m. & saw him kiss the Book: which awful ceremony ought certainly to keep your box straight. But to cover all risks I dine with W. on Friday & we will, further, drink to its health!–I met a few nights ago (at Palgrave's) your friend Gaskell & his wife—a very old-English beauty. Gaskell called on me 2 days since (I didn't see him), & I shall return his visit to day & hope to see something of him.[2] I spent yesterday most deliciously with Cunliffe at Hatfield—an enchanting June day & an ineffable place. I don't envy your being where you can't see it! The C.'s are leaving town & I shall miss them. I salute Mrs. Adams.

Yours very truly
H. James jr.

MS  MHS

1. The receipt from the American-European Express is still archived with the original letter. Dated June 5, 1877, it specifies: "One box said to contain paintings. Value one hundred pounds."

2. On June 22, 1877, Adams wrote to Charles Milnes Gaskell (1842–1919), his close friend since 1863 and a one-time M. P.: "Harry James writes me that you called on him of which I am glad, for I like him though I don't read his books. Some people admire them. If you ask him to Wenlock, you will I doubt not, find him much after your own taste. He would appreciate Wenlock, which is quite after his theory of life and imagination, so I hope you will try him" (Levenson *et al.*, eds., *Letters of Henry Adams*, II, 307). Gaskell had married Lady Catherine Henrietta Wallop (1856–1935) on December 7, 1876.

## 5 JAMES TO ADAMS

Wenlock Abbey,
Shropshire.
July 15th [1877][1]

My dear Adams—

Just before I left London came to me your letter giving news of the arrival of your case of drawings, which I was glad to hear were uninjured & to your taste. The expense of carriage was *not* paid in advance, & you have doubtless by this time been made responsible for it. All I paid was a trumpery sum to the consul, which I have forgotten, but which I will try & recollect when we meet. Very oddly at the same instant that I rec'd your letter, with its timely injunction to go to Wenlock should the occasion offer itself, came a gracious note from Lady Catherine Gaskell inviting me to the same enchanting spot. I was on the point of going abroad, but the coincidence of these solicitations seemed a thing not to be made light of; so I deferred my departure for two or three days, & came down here on the 12th ult. This is my last day, & I can't let it pass without thanking you for your share in bringing about so agreeable an episode. I had seen next to nothing of Gaskell & his wife in town. With him I had had but 10 minutes' talk, & Lady C. I had but admiringly looked upon. (I had been unable to accept their invitation to dinner.) It was therefore all the more meritorious in them to invite me hither, where they have come only for a week, to interrupt London & be alone. By this time I feel as if I know them almost well—as well, without the "almost," I certainly like them. Gaskell I find an excellent fellow, an entertaining companion & the pearl of hosts. We have talked together as people talk in an English country-house when, during the three days of a visit, two, alas, turn out too brutally pluvial. This is a rather big thorn on the Wenlock rose, which, however, on my first day, bloomed irreproachably. A rose without a thorn, moreover, is Lady Catherine G., of whom you asked for a description. I can't give you a trustworthy one, for I really think I am in love with her. She is a singularly charming creature—a perfect English beauty of the finest type. She is, as I suppose you know, very young, girlish, childish: she strikes me as having taken a long step straight from the governess-world into a particularly luxurious form of matrimony. She is very tall, rather awkward & not well made, wonderfully fresh & fair, expensively & picturesquely ill-dressed, charmingly mannered &, I should say, intensely in love with her husband. She would not in the least strike you at first as a beauty (save for complexion:) but presently you would agree with me that her face is a remarkable example of the classic English sweetness & tenderness—the thing that Shakspeare, Gainsborough, &c, may have meant to indicate. And this not at all stupidly—on the contrary, with a great deal of vivacity, spontaneity & cleverness. She says very good things, smiles adorably & appeals to her husband with beautiful inveteracy & naturalness. There is something very charming in seeing a woman in her pretty "position" so perfectly fresh & girlish. She will doubtless, some day, become more of a British matron or of a fine lady; but I suspect she will never lose (not after 20 London seasons) a certain bloom of shyness & softness.— But I am drawing not only a full-length, but a colossal, portrait.[2]— As for the place, you will know without my telling you what I think of that. This is a Sunday morning, with a great raw rain-storm howling outside; but though this unpleasantness has lasted 48 hrs. it has really not put me out of humour with Wenlock. The morning after my arrival, luckily, Gaskell & I started off & made an heroic day of it—a day I shall always remember most tenderly. We went to Ludlow, to Stokesay & to Shrewsbury & we saw them all in perfection. You spoke of Stokesay, & I found it of course a gem. We lay there on the grass in the delicious little *préau,* beside the wall, with every feature of the old place still solid & vivid around us, & I don't think that, as a sensation, I ever dropped back, for an hour, more effectually into the past.[3] Ludlow, too, is quite incomparable & Shrewsbury most capital. The whole thing made a delightful day. Gaskell had proposed another for the morrow, but I am sorry to say that the heavens *dis*posed, otherwise. There is, however, a very handsome entertainment in simply loafing—lounging about such an interesting old house as this. I imagine, from what G. tells me, that it is better now than when you saw it—has more of its ancient detail uncovered & disentangled. Gaskell also tells me to say that, in the very act of writing to you, he is deterred by the fact that I have got the start of him; so he keeps over his letter till he has the occasion to himself. He furthermore calls my attention to the screen you sent him on his marriage & which occupies a distinguished position in the drawing room, & bids me say that he & his wife consider it their handsomest appurtenance. It is indeed very handsome & "reflects great credit" as the newspapers say, on American workmanship. I pretend, patriotically, to Gaskell, that in America *nous n'en voyons pas d'autres*; but, in fact, I seem to myself to recognise in it the exceptional inspiration of your wife. But I must remember that my letter, though written on a rainy day, may not in your reading of it, under Beverly skies, have that assistance to your excusing its length.—I go back to London tomorrow, simply to pick up my luggage & depart for the continent, where I expect to spend 4 or 5 months in some quiet corner, favorable to work: at the end of which, D. V., I shall resume the thread of my British existence. I feel as if this thread had spun itself quite sufficiently thick to be, for the future, the main cable, as it were, that binds me to Europe. I appreciate your warning as to what that same future may lead to; & I know that, when the day comes, as I suppose it must, for snapping the cable, I shall need a very heroic tug. But I go on the plan that the safest remedy for the homesickness of after-years will have been to get all, & not less than all, one can now.

I had heard, from my brother Wm, of your ceasing your Cambridge work, & of the sort of labor & reputation that you are, as you say, going in for. May the former be as agreeable as the latter will doubtless be abundant![4] Even from Wenlock, London-and-(prospective)—Italy, I find a pulsation of my soul to envy you your Washington winter: but when it is over I shall find another to welcome you here. I hope your summer is a comfortable & happy one, & even believe it, knowing as I do in how rare a degree Beverly combines the charms of nature & of society!—But Lady Catherine comes in from the "chapel"—you remember the chapel—to inform me with her own rosy lips that lunch is being served. Commend me humbly to your wife, the memory of whose merits even the presence of those of Lady Catherine does not obscure,[5] & believe me very truly yours

*Henry James, jr.*

MS MHS

43

1. Printed in Edel, ed., *Henry James Letters*, II, 125–28.

2. On August 22, 1877, Adams wrote to Charles Milnes Gaskell: "Also let me now acknowledge and thank you for the photograph. It is very pretty but I had a prettier verbal one in a letter which Harry James wrote me from Wenlock and which drew a most graphic and pleasing picture of your situation. . . . I am glad you liked Harry James, and am glad you had him to Wenlock. I never read my friends' books, on principle, but am told his are not bad. His letters are excellent, and he professes the most touching sentiments toward your wife" (Levenson *et al.*, eds., *Letters of Henry Adams*, II, 315–16).

3. Not one to waste impressions, in "Abbeys and Castles," an essay published in *Lippincott's Magazine* in October, 1877, James wrote: "A friend of mine, an American, who knew this country, had told me not to fail, while I was in the neighbourhood, to go to Stokesay and two or three other places. 'Edward IV and Elizabeth,' he said, 'are still hanging about there.' So admonished, I made a point of going at least to Stokesay, and I saw quite what my friend meant. Edward IV and Elizabeth indeed are still to be met almost anywhere in the county; as regards domestic architecture few parts of England are still more vividly old-English. I have rarely had, for a couple of hours, the sensation of dropping back personally into the past so straight as while I lay on the grass beside the well in the little sunny court of this small castle and lazily appreciated the still definite details of medieval life" (Henry James, *English Hours*, ed. Alma Louise Lowe [New York, 1960], 146).

4. James refers to Adams' decision after seven years of teaching history at Harvard to move from Boston to Washington, D.C., where he could turn to a full-time writing career as a biographer and historian.

5. Adams would remember James's gallantry and adapt it to his own purposes. On October 6, 1878, he wrote to Gaskell: "If I am not already consumed by a wasting and fatal passion for Lady Catherine, to the despair of my wife and the destruction of our domestic peace, it is not the fault of the Gurneys nor of Harry James. I hope to survive, but not if you have many more of my friends at Wenlock" (Levenson *et al.*, eds., *Letters of Henry Adams*, II, 345–46).

## 6  JAMES TO ADAMS

3, Bolton Street,
Piccadilly, W.
[London]
May 5*th* [1879]

My dear Adams—

I am delighted to hear of the prospect of your so soon turning up on this side of the globe. I had heard it as a rumor, but your letter, this a.m. received, imparts reality to the vision. Arrive then as soon as possible—a warm welcome awaits you.[1] I shall be most happy to do anything in the world with regard to rooms for you, & I have a few general—very general—notions on the subject: but in default of a regular commission I don't feel justified in engaging a "fashionable suite" of apartments for you on the spot. You will have time after getting this to write to me to do so before you arrive, should you feel so inclined. You will arrive at a moment when, as a general theory, the best places are supposed to be occupied; but this promises to be a languishing & empty season, & I suppose that by the 1st of June there will still be a very good pick of lodgings. I don't, of my personal knowledge, know of anything particularly good, and as I got my dearest Gurneys last year into some rather inferior accommodations, I feel like proceeding now rather cautiously. All this region—this street & its neighbors, 1/2 Moon St. & Clarges St., are filled with apartments which I believe are supposed to be among the best in London. I went to 4 or 5 places in Clarges St. & 1/2 Moon St. after getting your note, to get a notion of the sort of thing that offered itself. There were some very good looking places (as London lodgings go,) where you could have a drawing-room & dining-room floor (i.e. four or five, or five or six rooms) for 12 or 13 guineas a week (very high!). Of course these places are liable to be taken from day to day. I will make the most diligent inquiry I can, between this & the end of the month, & if I hear from you by that time that you would like me to take something for you before you arrive I will religiously (tho' timorously) do so. Otherwise you will be able to descend at an inn & survey the field for yourself. But you had better *in the latter case* telegraph to me from Liverpool (or better, *Queenstown*) to secure places for you at an hotel.—Gaskell is abroad, where he has been for six weeks, or more; but he is expected back any day, I believe, & will take the highest interest in your arrival. My impression is that he intends taking a house in town for a couple of months; he spoke of it at lunch when I last saw him. I have seen a good deal of him first & last & have been both at Thornes & at Wenlock. His wife is altogether charming: I envy your making her acquaintance. I congratulate you on the completion (?) of your book.[2] I send the most cordial remembrances & good wishes to Mrs. Adams, I hold myself entirely at your service & I await with impatience your arrival. I have become such a thorough-haut Londoner, such a Piccadilly cockney, that I almost feel as if I cld. give you a sort of official welcome here. As I say, I will for the next three or four weeks ask for all the best information about lodgings; so that if you shld. wish me to nail a *gîte* for you, I shall be able to do something.[3] Always faithfully yours

*H. James jr.*

MS   MHS

1. Henry and Clover Adams sailed from New York on the *Gallia* on May 28, 1879, arriving in Queenstown on June 5.

2. James refers to Adams' *The Life of Albert Gallatin* (Philadelphia, 1879).

3. On May 21, 1879, Adams wrote to Gaskell: "We shall rest there a day or two [at Acton Park, Sir Robert Cunliffe's country seat] before going on to London, and I have asked Harry James to let me know there what hotel will take us in on reaching London" (Levenson *et al.*, eds., *Letters of Henry Adams*, II, 359).

## 7   JAMES TO MARIAN ADAMS

Lord Warden Hotel
Dover
Sept. *9th* [1880]

Dear Mrs. Adams.

Your favour just received. I am so glad you enjoyed the article on "Women in Organizations"—it must have been delightful reading for your hot weather.[1]—It has also been hot in this more temperate clime—which is a proximate cause of my having come down to this very quiet spot (where the quiet is extremely enjoyable,) to catch a sea-breeze. I shall probably be here till the 15th, & if you cross to Dover shall look out for you at the ship's side on that day. Why won't you stop here & see me? I will go up to London with you. A word to me in advance will secure you palatial rooms. I haven't much news for you as yet. I have been paying two or three short English visits, & am postponing Scotland till October. I shall at any rate see you in London, & see also I trust the seraphic robe, as well as the more terrestrial ones. But an angel in a *walking-costume*? I didn't know angels ever walked. You will be the first! I hear a good deal about the little book, *Democracy*, you mention—it was much talked of in Warwickshire, at Mrs. Carter's.[2] She, by the way, tho' yesterday the most disconsolate of widows, is immediately to marry E. L. Trevillian—your Washington Britisher.[3] He was staying at her house while I was there, & she announced me the fact with an abruptness which stunned me. Frailty, thy name!—is *not*

*H. J. jr.*

MS   MHS

    1. An essay by Kate Gannett Wells (1838–1911), "Women in Organizations" appeared in the *Atlantic Monthly*, XLVI (September, 1880), 360–67. It surveyed the social contributions women had made to professions, societies, and organizations.

    2. Published anonymously by Henry Holt in early 1880, *Democracy* was Henry Adams' satirical novel on politics in Washington. Just nine days earlier, on August 31, James had written to Thomas Sergeant Perry that he had "read *Democracy*, & thought it clever, though much of the satire a good deal too coarse. Who is it by, or attributed to?" he asked. "A man or a woman? It is good enough to make it a pity it isn't better" (Virginia Harlow, *Thomas Sergeant Perry: A Biography* [Durham, N.C., 1950], 309).

    3. James attended Mrs. Carter's wedding. To his sister on October 13, 1880, he wrote that he had spent an hour the day before "in a very cold church, to see my friend Mrs. Carter married: a rather dreary occasion, with a weeping bride, a sepulchral clergyman, who buried rather than married her, and a total destitution of relatives or accomplices of her own, so that she had to be given away by her late husband's brother!" (Edel, ed., *Henry James Letters*, II, 309).

## 8   JAMES TO MARIAN ADAMS

Cambridge
(20 Quincy St.)
Nov. 6*th*, 1881[1]

Dear Mrs. Adams.

    I wonder where I find courage (impudence you will perhaps call it) to write to you now, after having never written to you from the England you so cruelly deserted! I find it, I think, in the exhilaration of the prospect of soon seeing you in the Washington to which you so fondly cling—in the thought of the pleasant hours we shall pass there together,—in the vision of the social services which I know you will be so eager to render me! Your gracious promises of this kind linger serenely in my memory, & I find in them a pledge of delightful *intimate* weeks. I have been at home but a few days (since the 1st) but I cannot longer delay to let you know of my arrival—conscious as I am that it is fraught with happy consequences for you. I returned by way of Canada (in a ship of the Allan line) & getting off at a lonely village on the bank of the St. Lawrence, stole into the country, as it were, by the back-door. As therefore you may not have heard of my advent, these few lines will come to you with all the force of a delightful surprise. I am afraid, however, I shall not be with you (*with* you—I like that phrase!—) for a few weeks yet! When I do come, however, it will be to stay as long as possible. I remain another week or two at my father's—then go for a short time to Boston & N.Y.—then take the train for the sunny South. I remember so well your last charming words to me: "it will be over there that we shall really meet *familiarly*!" I must tell you that I am prepared to be intensely familiar! America seems to me delightful: partly perhaps because I have kept my rooms in Bolton St.! I shall bring you plenty of anecdotes—if your store has gone low. E. G. (in Paris, at a party) *An American gentleman* & H. J. jr. xxx.[2] *The A. G.* Did you read that charming little anonymous novel *Equality*?[3] Have you any idea who it's by?

*H. J. jr.* Not the smallest. But there are plenty of people over there—at least there are two or three—clever enough to have written it.

*The A. G.* No, it's not by an American—it can't be—from internal evidence.

*H. J. jr.* Internal evidence? xx

*The A. G.* There's a single word that betrays the writer's nationality. The princess is said to have worn *mock-lace*. Now that's a phrase the English always use. The Americans always say "*imitation-lace*." &c. &c.

I spent 10 days at Tillypronie not long before sailing—where there is always an uneasy curiosity xxxxx.[4] I should be so glad to have a word from you letting me know that you count on me now as I do on you! Love to Henry. Ever dear Mrs. Adams, impatiently & irrepressibly yours

*H. James jr.*

MS MHS

. Printed in Edel, ed., *Henry James Letters*, II, 361–62.
2. These *x*'s and those in the rest of the letter appear in the original.
3. A reference to Adams' novel *Democracy*.
4. Tillypronie (Aberdeenshire, Scotland) was the estate of Sir John Forbes Clark (1821–1910), a good friend to many Americans, including several members of Adams' circle.

## 9 JAMES TO ADAMS

115 East 25th Street
[New York]
Dec. 20*th* 1881

My dear Adams

Godkin spoke to me the other day of having got a letter from you in which you asked of news of me & expressed a kindly interest in the question of my arrival in Washington.[1] I have meant ever since to send you a personal answer to this inquiry—which should serve also as a response to the gracious note I received from your wife just after despatching her an [*sic*] (I trust) not less gracious one, three or four (five or six) weeks ago. I have been for the last three weeks the honoured guest of the master of this house, who has been showing me New York with great devotion & zeal. New York as exhibited by Godkin, is a very brilliant & hospitable city—we have dined out every day that he has not had a little party at home—& I have been almost lulled into oblivion of ulterior plans. But I am beginning to remember them now. I have not really relaxed at all my imaginative grasp upon Washington. Three days ago I should have told you that I expected to turn up there the 27th or 28th of the month; but I have just decided to go & spend Xmas at my father's, which (with another little delay,) will determine my advent for the 6*th* or 7*th* of January. I shall desire to take counsel with you of many things—be prepared therefore to be judicious. I am really waiting for Guiteau to be hanged—"we" order those matters better in England, where not only Guiteau, but Judge Cox, Mr. Scoville & everyone nearly or remotely concerned in the trial, would be delivered to the executioner.[2]

I enclose an elegant extract for your wife; & should like to know to what extent she deems it really compromising. Will the publication of such things really affect my social standing, & embarrass my human relations? &c.[3] If so I regret them, for I desire to live at peace with all the world. I hope you are living at peace, vous autres; & that you are having the same ethereal mildness. If your [sic] having the same, of course you are having greater. I embrace both & remain very faithfully yours

*Henry James jr.*

MS MHS

1. Edwin Lawrence Godkin (1831–1902) founded the *Nation* in 1865. On December 13, 1881, Adams wrote to Godkin: "We are expecting Harry James in Washington. When does he mean to come? Why don't you come? It's nonsense to say you can't. We can all do whatever is good for us" (Levenson *et al.*, eds., *Letters of Henry Adams*, II, 447).

2. Charles Guiteau, who was born in 1841, assassinated President James Garfield. Judge Walter Smith Cox (1826–1902) presided over the trial. George Scoville, who was married to Guiteau's sister Frances "Franky" M. Scoville, defended Guiteau. Guiteau was executed on June 30, 1882. Henry and Clover Adams attended the trial for one day and actually visited Guiteau in jail. Clover wrote to her father on December 11, 1881, offering him her opinion of some of the principals: "Mrs. Scoville is a nice, quiet, ladylike-looking woman. Thought she and I were the most respectable-looking women in court. As to the Court being unruly or disorderly, it's all nonsense. How Judge Cox keeps his gravity is a marvel, the beast's sallies are more than unjudicial muscles can stand. Judge Cox is a gentleman and a scholar and the newspaper critics a set of idiots. . . . He's [Guiteau's] a cunning, shrewd beast, deranged in a sense no doubt, but he miscalculated, believing he would murder Garfield and get off through the gratitude of the 'Stalwarts.' He told one of the doctors he 'thought he should go to Europe when the trial was over.' I don't wish to have it repeated that I shook hands with the accursed beast, without the context being given. Someone would write on that they 'were sorry to hear that I had asked Guiteau to tea'" (Thoron, ed., *Letters of Mrs. Henry Adams*, 308–10).

3. This extract is no longer with the letter and remains unidentified.

## 10  JAMES TO ADAMS

Cambridge
Dec. 27th, 1881.

Dear Adams.

Thank you for your Castilian offers! I shall avail myself of them with native eagerness, but also with Castilian discretion. I pant & pine for Washington, & am irritated at the series of accidents that have delayed my arrival there. This Xmas in the bosom of my family has been indispensable, however, as it has also been very enjoyable. But I have been a-visiting for the last four months (taking in the weeks that preceded my departure from England,) and my desire for a quiet corner of my own has at last become *ferocious*. If I can find such a corner in Washington, I will not answer for the brevity of my sojourn there, & if you shld by chance hear of a good set of rooms (sitting-room, bed-room & bath-room: the latter indispensable) I wish that in charity you would take them for me! I shld. be willing to pay a goodish price for something comfortable & independent. I don't mean of course seriously to saddle you with this commission—I only mean to say: please take notice. Perhaps I *shall* go so far as to ask you to bespeak a room at Wormley's Hotel for me the day before I arrive: (as I am told that after Jan. 1*st* Washington is very full.) I have not put my nose into Boston, nor shall do so, & have seen no one but my own people, & the Gurneys.[1]—I may have lost an opportunity in missing Guiteau, but can not believe I have lost a pleasure. I care for the newspapers only enough to loathe them—though that they are capable of superior moments is proved in the *Tribune* of Dec. 25*th*, p. 8, which has just been sent me.[2] I send a Castilian greeting to your gracious lady & remain very impatiently yours[3]

*Henry James jr.*

MS   MHS

1. Ellen Sturgis Hooper, Mrs. Henry Adams' sister, was married to Ephraim Whitman Gurney (1829–1886).
2. James refers to the New York *Tribune's* unsigned review of his novel *The*

*Portrait of a Lady* on Christmas Day. This handsome review was the work of their mutual friend John Hay.

3. Of James's play on the term *Castilian* throughout this letter, two possible explanations occur to me. First, it may refer to Isabella Stewart Gardner (1840–1924), commonly referred to as "Mrs. Jack" after her husband John L. Gardner. According to Leon Edel, "[James] always fell in with her [Isabella's] idea of 'queenship' by posing as her loyal courtier and writing letters filled with this particular kind of ironic flattery" (Edel, ed., *Henry James Letters*, II, 266). See James's letter to Adams of July 30, 1906 (given below), in which James refers to "Isabella of so much more than Castille—whose note I have answered even with the yearning of another Ferdinand." The second possible explanation is that it may refer to Victoria Sackville-West, the illegitimate daughter of Sir Lionel Sackville-West and a Spanish gypsy dancer. As James wrote to Sir John Clark on January 8, 1882: "Having been here but for a few days I haven't yet seen our British Minister, Sackville West; but he appears to be much liked, and he has a most attractive little ingénue of a daughter, the *bâtarde* of a Spanish ballerina, brought up in a Paris convent, and presented to the world for the first time here" (*Ibid.*, 367).

## 11   JAMES TO MARIAN ADAMS

131 Mt. Vernon St.
[Boston]
Feb. 28*th* [1883][1]

Dear Mrs. Adams.

It was very pleasant, the other day, to see your hand-writing, & it would be pleasanter still to see something more of you. If I were at liberty to take the proper course for doing so, I should start tomorrow for your milder latitude. But I am tied rather tight to Boston just now—being unable to go away & leave my sister companionless.[2] I don't despair however of spending a few days by the Potomac in April.—I see now the advantage last winter, of having discovered the situation of that stream. I sent you my little volume the other day rather as a compliment than with the expectation that you would approve of many of my points of view.[3] None of them, however, are my own—I can assure you of that. I am keeping my own for a grand ultimate work of fiction for which I expect the success in this country that *Democracy* has had in England. The latter work forms the favourite reading of Mr. Gladstone.[4] Mrs. Sands told me last summer that she had sat next to him at dinner, one day when he talked of it for an hour. "He said it was written in such a *handy* style, you know!" Trim your laurels, ye praised of prime ministers & professional beauties! You can imagine how I am enjoying my Boston Winter, & what a charming series of New Letters I am preparing. I lunch almost every Sunday with your sister at Cambridge—but the intervals are as flat as the New Land![5] I miss immensely your little douches of last winter—they at least produced a healthy glow & kept me alive. I should like very much some Washington gossip, but I don't make bold to ask you for any—you will say come & gossip yourself! I write this at the hour when I should naturally be sitting at your fireside, between Miss Beale & Miss Bayard possibly—if not between Miss Loring & the blonde widow who got me my rooms last year & whose name I have forgotten.[6] I find I am constantly much more disappointed than Miss Beale disappointed me & have now learned to give another name to the sensation she produced. As for Miss Bayard, since seeing her last year I have sought her like in vain in the Capitals of Europe. Il n'y a qu'elle!—& Miss West! You see in what a roseate vision Washington appears to me. I wonder whether you should be able to give me any news of Clarence King & of John Hay, of whom (both) I saw much last summer.[7] If not, I should give you some. Clarence is a truly festive nature, & has more water-colours even than you. Hay is less festive, for good reasons I fear; but very pleasant to talk with in Paris after dining with King! I *do* count seriously upon getting on to Washington for a little about six weeks hence; I think that will be a cozy moment. Keep a place warm for me—or so late in the spring, perhaps, keep it *cool*, & with friendliest remembrances to H. A. believe me ever faithfully

*Henry James*

MS MHS

1. Printed in Edel, ed., *Henry James Letters*, II, 407–408.
2. Alice James (1848–1892) would later move permanently to London.
3. James sent the volume entitled *The Siege of London, The Pension Beaurepas, and The Point of View* (Boston, 1883). Inscribed "Marian Adams/from the author/Feb 16—1883—," this copy is now in MHS.
4. William Ewart Gladstone (1809–1898) was four times England's prime minister.
5. Mrs. Adams' sister was Ellen Sturgis Gurney.

6. James's banter centers on Emily Beale, later Mrs. John Roll McLean and the model for the character Virginia Dare in Adams' *Democracy*; Katherine Bayard (1857–1886), the daughter of Thomas Francis Bayard, the senator from Delaware who would later become secretary of state and ambassador to the Court of St. James's and Mary Loring (1834–1905), whose name was sometimes put forth in the early 1880s as the author of *Democracy*. The "blonde widow" was, Mrs. Adams writes elsewhere, "an indefatigable white housekeeper who keeps her underlings scrubbing all day and it is as neat as wax" (Thoron, ed., *Letters of Mrs. Henry Adams*, 399).

7. Clarence King (1842–1901), a geologist and the author of the principal survey of natural resources in the United States, was one of Adams' closest friends. John Hay (1838–1905), poet, novelist, and biographer, later served as ambassador to the Court of St. James's and as United States secretary of state.


## 12 JAMES TO MARIAN ADAMS

> 3 Bolton St. W.
> [London]
> March 9*th* [1885]

Dear Mrs. Adams.

Your rustic note has the aroma of Lafayette Square as I inhaled that sweet fragrance for the last time, nearly two years ago. (I don't mean the very last time of all, for it is my firm intention to arrive in Washington about the year 1907, to pass the green old age, rich in reminiscence, for which I am preparing myself here.)[1] Mrs. Procter is *not* dying, alas, but her poor daughter Edythe, of a dismal, lingering, painful, malady, & it is apparently to be the old lady's fate to survive everyone, & everything, belonging to her, & to live to ninety.[2] (She is 85 or 86—& still extraordinarily attached to existence, grimly interested in it, & as ready to give the death-stab to Mr. Gladstone as she was ten years ago.) Mrs. Duncan Stewart passed away just a year ago; & I miss her very much.[3] I still see Mrs. Rogerson sometimes, whose husband is also dead & her daughter married, so that she has plenty of leisure to get up fancy-dinners at the East End, row on the river, & cultivate other energetic pursuits.[4] Three days hence I go with her to spend a morning at Newgate &

the old Bailey.[5] There is no knowing what one may come to, & we wish to inspect the premises in advance. Mrs. Lowell's death has led to my seeing much of Lowell, & I have spent various 1/2 hours and hours with him constantly, during the last several weeks. His simplicity is that of the babe unborn. His wife's death has been a great shock to him, but he bears it very reasonably, & feels how precarious, after this last attack of insanity (it was very bad) her future—& his—would have been.[6] The Wm Darwins are now staying with him.[7] He is expecting from day to day news of the appointment of his successor here by Mr. Cleveland, though I think he would be very glad to remain, not knowing what to do with himself now nor where to turn. He told me he could never again live—especially alone—at Elmwood; & when he is turned out here I can't in the least figure to myself his future. If the bolt hasn't descended before this reaches you, do exert yourself with Katie Bayard to let him stay.[8] It is a great loss to me not to be in Washington during her administration. I flatter myself if I were there she would give me some high office of state—I shld. remind her I once gave her some bonbons. I suppose all the cabinet are learning the guitar.

You may be interested to hear that I dined last night in the company of Mrs. Andrew Lang & Miss Mary Anderson.[9] Miss A. does tricks with cards, & Mrs. L. has written a novel, in a bright red cover.[10] Andrew writes for *Punch* & has presented her with a diamond locket out of the proceeds. Frk. Palgrave still comes in to see about 11 a.m. once in a while, & the last time brought with him the welcome news that he was going to Italy, for three months! He is selling his collection of drawings. Do you want to buy them? Lady Cathi Gaskell has become an authoress—writes in the reviews, & her brother Lymington has married a rich [grandduchess (?)] & gone to Australia.[11] The Gaskells have invited me, vainly, to Thornes, & *never* show themselves now in London. R. Cunliffe upholds an infirm & tottering administration, of which his support is, to me, the only agreeable feature. Mrs. Stanley Clarke mourns a husband absent in the Soudan,[12] & I am ever, with very friendly remembrances to the historian, very faithfully yours

*Henry James*

MS  MHS

1. James's prediction came close. He returned to the United States in 1904.

2. Anne Benson Procter (1799[?]–1888) was the widow of Waller Bryan Procter, the poet who wrote under the pseudonym Barry Cornwall.

3. Mrs. Duncan Stewart died in 1884. Clover Adams had written to her father on July 13, 1879: "Mr. James made me acquainted with a charming old lady, Irish by birth, Mrs. Duncan Stewart by name, who 'delighted, my dear, in Americans—they are all so charming!'" (Thoron, ed., *Letters of Mrs. Henry Adams*, 154).

4. Christina Rogerson, the widow of James Rogerson, was the daughter of Mrs. Duncan Stewart.

5. It is likely that James was still researching English prisons for an early scene in the novel he was then writing, *The Princess Casamassima*. A few months previously, he told Thomas Sergeant Perry in a letter dated December 12, 1884: "I have been all the morning at Millbank prison (horrible place) collecting notes for a fiction scene. You see I am quite the Naturalist" (Harlow, *Thomas Sergeant Perry*, 319).

6. Mrs. James Russell Lowell died suddenly in February, 1885.

7. William Darwin, the son of Charles Darwin, was married to Sara Sedgwick Darwin (1864–1922).

8. Katherine Bayard's father, Thomas Francis Bayard, as President Grover Cleveland's secretary of state (1885–1889), was officially in charge of the United States diplomatic corps. Earlier in the year, on January 24, James had written to Grace Norton: "Another drama interesting me is the question of poor dear J. R. Lowell's possible recall after Cleveland mounts the throne. This, to me, is tragic, pathetic. His position here is in the highest degree honourable, useful, agreeable— in short perfect; and to give it all up to return, from one day to another, to John Holmes and the Brattle Street horsecar (which is very much what it amounts to— save when he goes to see you,) seems to me to be the sport of a cruel, a barbaric, fortune" (Edel, ed., *Henry James Letters*, III, 67). Lowell was replaced.

9. Mary Anderson (1859–1940) was an American actress and an old friend of James's.

10. Mrs. Leonore Blanche Lang's novel in two volumes was *Dissolving Views*, published in 1884 by Harpers in New York and Longmans in London.

11. Lady Catherine's brother was Newton Wallop (1856–1917), Viscount Lymington.

12. Mary Temple Rose, the daughter of Sir John Rose and Charlotte Temple Rose and the wife of Colonel Stanley Clarke, equerry to the Prince of Wales, was James's distant cousin. She died in 1913. James's story "The Marriages" (1891) is based on Mrs. Clarke's unhappy reaction to her father's intention to remarry; see Edel and Powers, eds., *Notebooks*, 32–33.

## 13  JAMES TO ADAMS

Hotel de Sienne
Siena
June 15th [1892]

My dear Adams.

Lefautau's little letter is charming—Lefautau's and Ariimanihi-nihi's—and I thank you kindly for having transmitted it. It is the consequence of an envoi to ces dames of a couple of "author's presentation" copies of my books at the behest of John LaFarge.[1] It makes me feel famous—& doesn't discourage that psychological lust—au contraire—on which you freely animadvert & to the exercise of which, precisely, I appear to owe it that I can brandish such trophies. Besides I am in a tainted air just now (for that sort of renunciation;) having come to spend the month of June in this admirable old city *auprès* of my ingenious friend Paul Bourget (& his charming young Tanagra-statuette wife,) from whom exudes the vicious principle at every pore.[2] But anything for a change. My brother is at Freiburg in Breisgau—but summers apparently in Switzerland, where I ultimately join him. You really must come down from the Seaside to lunch with me sometime in September. I shall be sorry not to see you. I spend the summer presumably abroad, but London in its sweet desolation will eventually call me. I may even be back in August. Stia bene.

*Ever yours*
*Henry James*

P.S. *Can't* you bring King?[3]

MS  MHS

1. John La Farge (1835–1910), the artist, was one of James's early Newport friends. La Farge was accompanied by Adams in his South Seas journeys in the early 1890s. In *Reminiscences of the South Seas* (New York, 1912), La Farge refers to the Tahitian "Miss Manihinihi." He writes: "Queen Marau has been very affable and entertaining, telling us legends and stories; Miss Piri has been ailing, Miss Chiki, smiling. The women of the family are all extremely interesting, of various types, but each one with a charm of her own; from Marau's strong face, fit for a queen, to Manihinihi's bright cordial smile. And such beautiful voices as they have, and rich

intonation! It is a remarkable family and a princely one" (p. 320). It is not known which of James's books he sent on to the two women. But the only book he published within the two years prior to the date of this letter was *The Lesson of the Master*, published in February, 1892.

2. Of Paul Bourget (1852–1935), the French essayist and novelist, and of his young wife Minnie, James wrote to Charles Eliot Norton on July 4, 1892: "My friends were Paul Bourget . . . and his very remarkably charming, cultivated and interesting young wife. They have been living in Italy these two years—ever since their marriage, and I have been living much *with* them here. Bourget is a very interesting mind—and figure altogether—and the first—easily, to my sense—of all the talkers I have ever encountered. But it would take me much too far to *begin* to give you a portrait of such a complicated cosmopolitan Frenchman as he!" (Edel, ed., *Henry James Letters*, III, 387).

3. James had met Clarence King in London in 1882 and again shortly thereafter in the company of John Hay in Paris. To James, King was "the most delightful man in the world," though he was also "slippery and elusive, and as unmanageable as he is delightful" (Edel, *Henry James: The Treacherous Years*, 237). At King's death in 1901 John Hay wrote to Adams: "There you have it in the face! . . . the best and brightest man of his generation, with talents immeasurably beyond any of his contemporaries; with industry that has often sickened me to witness it; with everything in his favor but blind luck; hounded by disaster from his cradle, with none of the joy of life to which he was entitled, dying at last, with nameless suffering, alone and uncared-for, in a California tavern. *Ça vous amuse, la vie?*" (Quoted in Henry Adams, *The Education of Henry Adams* [Boston, 1918], 416).

## 14  JAMES TO ADAMS

Osborne Hotel
Torquay.
Thursday.
[Oct. (?) 1895][1]

My dear Henry!

This is very sad; for I haven't the least hope that you'll come down here. On the other hand I can't come up if I would, having nowhere to lay my head. My rooms are choked with paperers, painters & ~~elet~~ (I can't spell it!) electric lighters, & *ils en out* for a month. So the end is not yet. I'm very, very sorry to miss you: you periodically prepare me for that reaction in favour of my lone exile to which I owe it, I think, that I hobble on. The only thing is that the periods are too interspaced; & I much deplore missing this one altogether. Come back, come back. I don't say, "Come down, come down"—only because the responsibility is too great, & my little Crescent, with its green lawn & its blue water, too liable, through true Devonshire dulness, to be placed by you in the light even too lurid to be reacted in favour of! (With Devonshire dulness I am acquiring Devonshire English.) I have been here since the 20*th* July— & have wondered much about you.[2] I hope your summer has been impressionistic & your clothing light. There was much I wanted to hear from you. Alas! Do try me again; & believe me yours, my dear Adams, from long ago

*Henry James*

MS   MHS

1. Adams himself dates the letter "Oct. 1895."
2. Adams, along with Nanny and Henry Cabot Lodge, had been in London from mid-July to early August but returned early in October for a few days. By the end of the month he was back in Washington. James's stay in Devonshire, interrupted by a short return to London in August, lasted until early November. (See Edel, *Henry James: The Treacherous Years*, 140–53, and Cater, ed., *Henry Adams and His Friends*, 341–51.)

## 15   ADAMS TO JAMES

> 23 Avenue du Bois
> de Boulogne
> [Paris]
> 18 Nov. 1903.[1]

My dear James

Although you, like most men of toil, hate to be bored, I can hardly pass over your last work without boring you to the extent of a letter.[2] We have reached a time of solar antiquity when nothing matters, but still we feel what used to be called the law of gravitation, mass, or attraction, and obey it.

More than ever, after devouring your William Story, I feel how difficult a job was imposed on you. It is a *tour de force*, of course, but that you knew from the first. Whether you have succeeded or not, I cannot say, because it all spreads itself out as though I had written it, and I feel where you are walking on firm ground, and where you are on thin ice, as though I were in your place. Verily I believe I wrote it. Except your specialty of style, it is me.

The painful truth is that all of my New England generation, counting the half-century, 1820–1870, were in actual fact only one mind and nature; the individual was a facet of Boston. We knew each other to the last nervous centre, and feared each other's knowledge. We looked through each other like microscopes. There was absolutely nothing in us that we did not understand merely by looking in the eye. There was hardly a difference even in depth, for Harvard College and Unitarianism kept us all shallow. We knew nothing—no! but really nothing! of the world. One cannot exaggerate the profundity of ignorance of Story in becoming a sculptor, or Sumner in becoming a statesman, or Emerson in becoming a philosopher. Story and Sumner, Emerson and Alcott, Lowell and Longfellow, Hillard, Winthrop, Motley, Prescott, and all the rest, were the same mind,—and so, poor worm!—was I![3]

Type bourgeois-bostonien! A type quite as good as another, but more uniform.[4] What you say of Story is at bottom exactly what you would say of Lowell, Motley, and Sumner, barring degrees of egotism. You cannot help smiling at them, but you smile at us all equally. God knows that we knew our want of knowledge! the self-distrust became introspection—nervous self-consciousness—irritable dislike of America, and antipathy to Boston. *Auch ich* war in Arcadien geboren!

So you have written not Story's life, but your own and mine,— pure autobiography,—the more keen for what is beneath, implied, intelligible only to me, and half a dozen other people still living: like Frank Boott; who knew our Boston, London and Rome in the fifties and sixties.[5] You make me curl up, like a trodden-on worm. Improvised Europeans, we were, and—Lord God!—how thin! No, but it is too cruel! Long ago,—at least thirty years ago,—I discovered it, and have painfully held my tongue about it. You strip us, gently and kindly, like a surgeon, and I feel your knife in my ribs.

No one else will ever know it. You have been extremely tactful. The essential superficiality of Story and all the rest, you have made painfully clear to us, but not, I think, to the family or the public. After all, the greatest men are weak. Morley's Gladstone is hardly thicker than your Story.[6] Let us pray!

*Ever Yrs*
*Henry Adams*

MS HL

1. Printed in Worthington Chauncey Ford, ed., *Letters of Henry Adams (1892–1918)* (Boston, 1938), 413–15; Newton Arvin, ed., *Selected Letters of Henry Adams* (New York, 1951), 239–40; and Levenson *et al.*, eds., *Letters of Henry Adams*, V, 523–24.

2. James's *William Wetmore Story and His Friends* (1903) was published in Edinburgh and London by William Blackwood and in Boston by Houghton Mifflin.

3. Adams ticks off the following individuals who are of "one mind": (1) William Wetmore Story (1819–1895), sculptor, essayist, and poet, who in mid-life left Boston and a successful career in law for Rome and a career in the arts; (2) Charles Sumner (1811–1874), United States senator from Massachusetts; (3) Ralph Waldo Emerson (1803–1882), poet and philosopher; (4) Amos Bronson Alcott (1799–1888), educator, author, mystic, and (according to the *Dictionary of American Biography*) "the most transcendentalist of the Transcendentalists"; (5) James Russell Lowell (1819–1891), author, teacher, diplomat, and (again according to the *DAB*) the "foremost American man of letters" of his time; (6) Henry Wadsworth Longfellow (1807–1882), poet; (7) George Stillman Hillard (1808–1879), lawyer and writer; (8) Robert Charles Winthrop (1809–1894), representative and senator from Massachusetts; John Lothrop Motley (1814–1877), diplomat and historian; and (9) William Hickling Prescott (1796–1859), historian.

4. Adams reacts directly to James's observations on Story's visit in 1855 to Boston, which Story found to be superficially "bourgeois." James wrote: "His chagrin, it need scarcely, after all, be added, was eminently 'subjective.' . . . What it all came to saying, however, was that, with an alienated mind, he found himself again steeped in a society both fundamentally and superficially *bourgeois*, the very type and model of such a society, presenting it in the most favourable, in the most admirable light; so that its very virtues irritated him, so that its ability to be strenuous without passion, its cultivation of its serenity, its presentation of a surface on which it would appear to him that the only ruffle was an occasionally acuter spasm of the moral sense, must have acted as a tacit reproach" (Henry James, *William Wetmore Story and His Friends* [Boston, 1903], I, 303–304).

5. Francis Boott (1813–1904), a composer, was the father of James's friend Lizzie Boott, who is thought to be James's model for Pansy, Gilbert Osmond's daughter in *The Portrait of a Lady*.

6. To John Hay on November 22, 1903 (just four days after his letter to James), Adams wrote: "Please read Harry James's Life of Story! Also Morley's Gladstone! And reflect—wretched man!—that now you have knowingly forced yourself to be biographised! You cannot escape the biographer" (Levenson *et al.*, eds., *Letters of*

*Henry Adams*, V, 526). Years later Adams was still talking about James's *Story*. To his brother Brooks he wrote on February 18, 1909: "Failure matters little when it concerns only oneself. Henry James can fail as often as he likes in novels, but when he fails in biography, he leaves mighty little of William Story. In biography we are taking life" (*Ibid.*, VI, 227).

## 16  JAMES TO ADAMS

Lamb House, Rye,
Sussex.
November 19*th* 1903[1]

My dear Adams.

I am so happy at hearing from you *at all* that the sense of the particular occasion of my doing so is almost submerged & smothered. You did bravely well to write—make a note of the act, for your future career, as belonging to a class of impulses to be precipitately obeyed &, if possible, even tenderly nursed. Yet it has been interesting, exceedingly, in the narrower sense, as well as delightful in the larger, to have your letter, with its so ingenious expression of the effects on you of poor *W. W. S.*—with whom, & the whole business of whom, there is (yes, I can see!) a kind of *inevitableness* in my having made you squirm—or whatever is the proper noun for the sensation engendered in you! Very curious, & even rather terrible, this so far-reaching action of a little biographical vividness— which did indeed, in a manner, begin with me, myself, even as I put the stuff together—though pushing me to conclusions less grim, as I may call them, than in your case. The truth is that *any* retraced story of bourgeois lives (lives other than great lives of "action"—*et encore!*) throws a chill upon the scene, the time, the subject, the small mapped-out facts, & if you find "great men thin" it isn't really so much their fault (& least of all yours) as that the art of the biographer—devilish art!—is somehow practically *thinning*. It simplifies even while seeking to enrich—& even the Immortal are so helpless & passive in death. The proof is that I wanted to invest dear old Boston with a mellow, a golden glow—& that for those who know, like yourself, I only make it bleak—& weak! Luckily those who know are indeed but three or four—& they won't, I hope, too promiscuously tell. For the book, meanwhile, I seem to learn, is much acclaimed in the U.S.—a better fate than I hoped for the mere dissimulated-perfunctory.[2] The Waldo Storys absolutely *thrust* the job upon me five, six, *seven* years ago—& I had been but dodging & delaying in despair at the meagerness of the material (*every*—documentary—scrap of which I have had thriftily to make use of.) At last I seemed to see a *basis*—of subjective amplification—by which something in the nature of a *book* might be made, & then I could with some promptness work my little oracle.[3] Someone has just written to ask me if the family "like it", & I have replied that I think they don't know whether they like it or not! They are waiting to find out—& I am glad on the whole they haven't access to *you*. I wish I myself had—beyond *this*. But even this, as I tell you, has been a great pleasure to yours, my dear Adams, always & ever

*Henry James*

MS  MHS

1. Printed in Lubbock, ed., *Letters of Henry James*, I, 431–32 (with ellipses); Edel, ed., *Henry James Letters*, IV, 288–89; and Edel, ed., *Selected Letters of Henry James* (1987) 349–50.

2. James's biographer writes that "certain of his [James's] critics in the United States described the Story volumes as the 'sacrifice' of a fine subject to Henry James's egotism. The statement was true" (Leon Edel, *Henry James: The Master, 1901–1916* [Philadelphia, 1972], 159). And Richard Nicholas Foley tells us that most of the reviews of the book were not more than "brief, complimentary comments" (Foley, *Criticism in American Periodicals of the Works of Henry James from 1866 to 1916* [Washington, D.C., 1944], 90). But Linda J. Taylor's meticulous investigation of the contemporary reviews of *William Wetmore Story and His Friends* upholds James's assertion that the book was "much acclaimed in the U.S." (Taylor, *Henry James, 1866–1916: A Reference Guide* [Boston, Mass., 1982], 330–45).

3. On January 25, 1902, James had complained revealingly to his friend William Dean Howells: "[I] suffered to be gouged out of me long ago by the Waldo Storys— a history in itself—a promise first to 'look at' the late W. W. S[tory]'s papers and then to write a memorial volume of some sort about him. I've delayed quite desperately, and at last, quite *must*, as I've also promised Wm Blackwood here. But there is no *subject*—there is nothing in the man himself to write about. There is nothing for me but to do a *tour de force*, or try to—leave poor dear W. W. S. *out*, practically, and make a little volume on the old Roman, Americo-Roman, Hawthornesque and other bygone days, that the intending, and extending, tourist will, in his millions, buy. But pray for me *you*, over this—to do all that and Please the Family too! Fortu-

nately the Family is almost cynically indulgent—and I hope not to be kept Pleasing it more than three or four months. But my lamp burns low" (Edel, ed., *Henry James Letters*, IV, 224–25). To the Duchess of Sutherland, on December 23, 1903, however, he wrote: "Story was the dearest of men, but he wasn't massive, his artistic and literary baggage were of the slightest and the materials for a biography *nil*. Hence (once I had succumbed to the amiable pressure of his children), I had really to *invent* a book, patching the thing together and eking it out with barefaced irrelevancies— starting above all *any* hare, however small, that might lurk by the way. It is very pleasant to get from a discriminating reader the token that I have carried the trick through" (*Ibid.*, IV, 302). James's letter did not cause Adams to change his mind. See note 6 to previous letter.

## 17   JAMES TO ADAMS

95 Irving St.
Cambridge, Mass.
11.24.1904

My dear Adams.

Very noble & beautiful your letter, by which please believe that I am infinitely touched. Nothing could be more delightful to me than to pay you a visit in Washington, & my heart leaps up at the thought—so that I should have been almost capable indeed of a direct *appeal* to your hospitality in advance. But a certain amount of waiting, for these superior joys has been imposed upon me, & the ordeal of patience has been in order. I have had to make sure, here, of a decent visit to my brother (with whom I had previously been but for some days in the country) before launching out on wider waters—& an interminable siege with the dentist (cursed be the race!) is making this longer than I had quite intended. I go as early as I can manage next month (but not, I fear, before the 10*th*) to make a stay of some duration in New York—having had it at heart to clear the ground, so to speak, *préalablement* of that city, which has seemed to block my way to Washington. But as soon as I have dealt with it I shall proceed straight into your presence, & I will let you know as much as possible in advance the date of my being able to do so. I have an idea—possibly presumptuous—that you are always a part of

your year in Paris—& perhaps are even in the habit of going there
before the winter is over: wherefore I would, should your departure
be coming into sight, come on to Washington earlier, & make a
point of it, in order not to miss you. I shall be in the U.S. (D. V.) as
late as June or July, & have been cultivating the idea of a certain
method & logic—even to subtlety!—in my sequences—& if you are
not migrating (as I earnestly hope,) shall see you at home some time
(the earlier the better,) in February. Give, very aboundingly, please,
to Hay, the assurance of my affectionate constancy: deep is my desire
to grasp him by the hand, but subject, thus, to a horrid, a monstrous, an inevitable regulation. Let me give you of my news again,
before too long, in more definitely responsive form, &
believe me, my dear Adams, yours always & ever

*Henry James*

MS MHS


## 18   JAMES TO ADAMS

21, East Eleventh<br>Street.<br>[New York]<br>December 23d 1904.

My dear Henry.

    I am in receipt of great benevolence from you—through, 1st, the
grace of Mrs. Cameron, &, 2d, that of your letter.[1] I go to Philadelphia for one night on the 9th, & proceed thence to Washington at
some such hour on Tuesday 10th as will permit my arriving conve-
niently for dinner. I have the honour of partaking of that meal that
evening with the Hays, but I shall be delighted to descendre chez
vous precedently, & if you can put me up till the following Monday
or Tuesday I shall think myself blest. I shall *have* to come away then,
in all probability, but shall be able to return early in February for
another fortnight or so. There comes to me as I write an invitation
from Charles McKim to attend an Architectural Dinner on the 11th

& I am thinking of accepting it for local colour's sake & *gentilesse* to McKim;[2] but after that I shall be very entirely yours

Henry James

MS MHS

1. Elizabeth Sherman Cameron (1857–1944), the wife of Senator James Donald Cameron, was one of Adams' closest friends.

2. James did attend the famous dinner given by Charles Follen McKim (1847–1909) under the auspices of the American Institute of Architects at the Arlington Hotel the evening of January 11, 1905. An account of this event is given in Charles Moore, *The Life and Times of Charles Follen McKim* (Boston, 1929), 242–46. James appreciated the attention accorded him but had reservations about the event itself, for he wrote that the dinner was "a big success and beautifully done—but the Eagle screamed in the speeches and I didn't know that that fowl was still (after all these years and improvements,) *permitted* to do. It was werry werry quaint and queer—but so is *everything, sans exception,* and the sensitive Célimare absorbs it at every pore" (Edel, *Henry James: The Master,* 266). Célimare, the name of a character out of a French farce, was Mrs. Mary Cadwalader Rawle "Minnie" Jones's pet name for James. James was then staying at the New York home of Mrs. Jones, who was married to Edith Wharton's brother Frederic Rhinelander Jones.

## 19   JAMES TO ADAMS

884 Park Avenue.
N.Y. City.[1]
Jan: 7: 1905

My dear Henry!

Only a word to say that, yes, very positively & rejoicingly, I present myself at your door on Tuesday afternoon next 9*th*. I come on from Philadelphia, where I shall have passed Monday evening & night (Rittenhouse Club, 1811 Walnut St.,) & don't know as yet about trains, but I shall do my best to reach you as nearly as possible at "tea-time."[2] Mrs. Cameron dined here last night (Mrs. Wharton's) very radiantly, & I am yours always

Henry James

MS MHS

1. The address is that of James's fellow novelist and friend Edith Wharton (1862–1937).

2. On January 9, 1905, James presented the lecture "The Lesson of Balzac" to the Contemporary Club of Philadelphia. He arrived in Washington on the tenth, not the ninth (see Edel, ed., *Henry James Letters*, IV, 336).

## 20  JAMES TO ADAMS

Jefferson Hotel
Richmond, Va.
Feb: 1: 1905[1]

My dear Henry.

I have written 1st to thank R. U. Johnson for crowning me with glory—& now I must thank *you* for guiding, straight to my unworthy & even slightly bewildered brow, his perhaps otherwise faltering or reluctant hand.[2] Well, I am crowned—& I don't know that that makes much difference; but, still more, I am *amused,* & that very certainly does—the amazement the more, in the somewhat stale dream of existence, & suddenly clapped down before one, & for which there is nothing to pay—& which may go on & on & develop a richness all its own: this surely is more than one had seemed to one's self to be hoping for—& the charming list, already, seems to flush with the promise. I rejoice in the thought that it will, be longer—for the amusement must now be in exact proportion to its length. There are *candidatures* I am waiting for—& altogether this dreary place, where I arrived last night, on my diabolical journey (with a *harvest* of sweet impressions from Philadelphia) is quite warmed & lighted up by your contribution. Still, I am homesick, on my way to Florida—for the evenings when I used to listen to Moreton Frewen—& to wish he were Mrs. Lodge.[3] But, good-night cher confrere. I hope you are thinking of our uniform. But keep it cheap—think what Theodore will want.[4] Yours academically

*Henry James*

MS MHS

1. Printed in Edel, ed., *Henry James Letters*, IV, 343.
2. Robert Underwood Johnson (1853–1937), an editor of the *Century* and at the time secretary to the National Institute of Arts and Letters, had announced the

second-round election of James and Adams to the American Academy of Arts and Letters.

3. Moreton Frewen (1853–1924) was an English friend of Adams', James's, and Stephen Crane's (Crane lived in Frewen's Brede Place in the last year of his life). Frewen was in Washington championing bimetallism, a lifelong passion. Mrs. Lodge was probably Matilda Elizabeth Frelinghuysen Davis, the wife of George Cabot "Bay" Lodge.

4. President Theodore Roosevelt, who in his time was well known and much honored for his writing, was elected to the academy at the same time as Adams and James. See George Monteiro, "Henry James and the American Academy of Arts and Letters," *New England Quarterly,* XXXVI (March, 1963), 82–84.

## 21  JAMES TO ADAMS

1810 South
Rittenhouse Square.[1]
[Philadelphia]
2.22.05.

My dear Henry.

I committed the gross inadvertence of coming off from Washington with my latchkey, of your house door, in my pocket, & have only just become aware of the dereliction. Please find it enclosed, with my blessing & my contrition. I am up to my neck in the hospitality of this too, too genial city—too too solid flesh—or I would write you with a freer hand. The sense of Philadelphia rises to my chin, & I feel wedged (the most comfortably in the world, du reste,) tight into it. It is a thing by itself—though that isn't a thing it makes its recipient. I am a thing by myself barely long enough to scratch you three words. I pine a little for the larger issues of your wonderful talk-centre—& the rich tones of Morton [sic] Frewen linger desirably on my ear. But I spent yesterday a.m. in Independence Hall with Weir Mitchell & the p.m. with 3 or 4 select murderers in the Penitentiary.[2] Yet I *hadn't* murdered W. M. Give my love, please, to the Hays & to Mrs. Lodge, to Mrs. Lodge & the Hays & the Bays. Keep the key *for* me a little—dark, so dark, tho' the future—& believe me always yours

*Henry James*

MS MHS

1. The address was that of Dr. J. William White (1850–1916), a well-known surgeon.

2. Dr. Silas Weir Mitchell (1829–1914), a neurologist, was the author of several novels, perhaps the best known of which was *Hugh Wynne: Free Quaker* (1898).

## 22  JAMES TO ADAMS

Lamb House, Rye,
Sussex.
7.30.06.

My dear Henry!

It is most kind of you to have sent me on the behest of Isabella of so much more than Castille—whose note I have answered even with the yearning of another Ferdinand.[1] She has been at this place—stayed here some years since, very kindly—for a day—but it has conceivably faded from her soul. You are enough my neighbour to make me wish you were more so, & also that in spite of being almost *on* it, I had not unlearned so, of late years, the way to Paris—especially in these canicular weeks, when I hug the shade of my vine & fig tree. I grieve to read what you tell me of John LaFarge, & ask myself why, in such conditions, he wanders over the globe—neglecting *his* vine and fig tree—in opposition to my example! But please don't tell him I say this—only that I send him my love. It comes to me that his son Bancel is (to the best of my impression) there—so that I dearestly hope the felt pressure of his presence isn't felt *all* by you—capable as you are of accepting the lion's share of it.[2]

You have perhaps forgotten, in your princely generosity, that you made me a present, a year & a half ago, in Washington, of your sublime study of Mt. St. Michel & Chartres—which it has again & again sickened me [to] think I have till this hour not acknowledged the divine beauty & interest of.[3] While I remained in the U.S. I had absolutely no freedom of time nor of mind for it—nor at *first* after I came back here. But I have of late, after much frustration, been reading you with the bated breath of wonder, sympathy & applause. May I say, all unworthy & incompetent, what honour I think the beautiful volume does you & of how exquisite & distinguished an interest I have found it, with its easy lucidity, its saturation with its subject, its charmingly taken and kept, *tone*. Even more than I congratulate you on the book I envy you your relation to the subject. I suppose it vain for me to exhale the wish that you might come for a little to England. Vale! Yours, my dear Adams, very constantly & gratefully

*Henry James*

MS MHS

1. James refers to Isabella Stewart (Mrs. John) Gardner, who is best remembered for her Fenway Court, a Venetian palace, in Boston. To James, "Mrs. Jack," as he was wont to call her to friends, gave her name to the age: "the age of Mrs. Jack, the figure of Mrs. Jack, the American, the nightmare—the individual consciousness—the mad, ghastly climax or denouement" (Edel and Powers, eds., *Notebooks*, 126).
2. Bancel La Farge (1865–1938) was married to Adams' niece, Mabel Hooper.
3. Printed privately in Washington, D.C., in 1904, *Mont-Saint-Michel and Chartes* was not brought out for public sale until 1913, when it was published for the benefit of the American Institute of Architects.

## 23  JAMES TO ADAMS

Lamb House, Rye,
Sussex.
February 22d—
1907.[1]

My dear Henry.

Mrs. Hay has written to me, & returning to this place after a longish time in London, I have instituted an immediate search for such letters of dear J.H.'s as I might be able to find.[2] I didn't expect to find many, because our correspondence was never in a high degree active—very limited & occasional indeed; but I thought I might find more than the five notes I send you. There were a few—a very few—others of earlier years, & I had them, kept them for much of the after-time; but things *go,* strangely, with mood & vicissitudes—

so that I offer you meagre tribute. Very welcome you are to any word any one of these may contain—though that will strike you as almost nothing. I am very glad you are gathering in a selection, as I understand you to be doing, of Hay's letters—it will make the best form of commemorative record of his high wit, ability & character, & no one but you of course, should do it. I wish you all prosperity & send you all sympathy, in the business. If I can help you in any manner whatever at any ulterior stage I should be delighted. I go to Paris for some weeks a dozen days since—& should so rejoice if you were likely to turn up there before my retreat. I go for a short time also to Italy. I hope you are bearing up under—well under everything—& am yours very constantly

*Henry James*

MS LC

1. Printed in George Monteiro, "An Unpublished Henry James Letter," *Notes and Queries*, n.s., X (April, 1963), 143–44, and Monteiro, *Henry James and John Hay*, 136–37.
2. Clara Stone Hay (1839–1914) was the widow of John Hay (J.H.), who had died on July 1, 1905. At the request of Mrs. Hay, Adams was collecting Hay's letters for use in a commemorative volume. When privately printed in Washington, D.C., in 1908, *Letters of John Hay and Extracts from Diary* ran to three volumes. For a commentary on Adams' contribution to this project, see Philip B. Eppard, "Henry Adams and the Letters and Diaries of John Hay," *Books at Brown*, XXIX–XXX (1982–83), 119–28.

## 24  ADAMS TO JAMES

> 23 Avenue du Bois
> de Boulogne
> [Paris]
> 6 July. '07[1]

My dear James

I am sorry to have missed your visit, for I had hoped to see you quietly as of old; but I seem to see nothing any longer as of old, and I suppose the fault is in me, though the speed is not. If you enjoyed your Italy, I have no complaint to make, even of myself; though my own late visits to Italy have been rather in the nature of floggings. You would have got a sniff of youth and fun if you had practised the Latin Quarter a little with your nephew, where they are as young as they were in the Second Empire, and—as I maintain—don't know a good wine from a bad one.[2]

Come again! Ever yrs

*Henry Adams*

MS HL

1. Printed in Ford, ed., *Letters of Henry Adams (1892–1918)*, 481, and Levenson *et al.*, eds., *Letters of Henry Adams*, VI, 76.
2. The nephew was William James (1882–1961), William's son. The uncle and the nephew spent several weeks that spring traveling in Europe.

---

## 25 JAMES TO ADAMS

Lamb House, Rye,
Sussex.
July 8*th* 1907.

My dear Henry!

I am much touched by your kind letter. I could only *chance* you the other day in Paris[.] I was there but three [*sic*], on my way back from Italy—& I blush at having had to be so barbarous as to *brûler cette étape*. But I had been there 10 weeks in the Spring—when *you* were not, alas, & after 4 months away from home was so impatient to get back to neglected & urgent occupations that every day & every hour counted. I had literally not another to spare. Otherwise I would have renewed, to a certainty, my pilgrimage to your tower-top. I wish you sometimes came to England, though I don't recommend it unless you should come to "live"—it being to my mind (& contrary to the usual view) an excellent, the best, country to inhabit, but not so good a one for "staying." My time in France this year has however re-opened my appetite for that *séjour* & I very earnestly hope for another chance to gape at your wondrous avenue. It was of

a beauty the other afternoon!—& I kind of yearned to stay too. But
Peace is here, & I am ever so pacifically & faithfully yours

Henry James

MS MHS

<hr>

26 ADAMS TO JAMES

<hr>

23 Avenue du Bois
de Boulogne
[Paris]
6 May. 1908[1]

Mon cher Jacques

Mea culpa! Peccavi! Parce, frater! It is but a form and a phrase,
yet this volume is supposed to be lent out only for correction, suggestion and amendment, so that you are invited to return it, with
your marginal comments whenever you have done with it—I need
hardly tell *you* that my own marginal comment is broader than that
of any reader, and precludes publication altogether. The volume is a
mere shield of protection in the grave. I advise you to take your own
life in the same way, in order to prevent biographers from taking it
in theirs.[2]

Also—you being a literary artist, and therefore worth the
trouble of fore-warning—I note for your exclusive use the intent of
the literary artist—c'est moi!—to make this volume a completion
and mathematical conclusion from the previous volume about the
Thirteenth Century,—the three concluding chapters of this being
only a working out to Q.E.D. of the three concluding chapters
of that.[3] This is only for my own horizon; not for your confusion.
Ever yrs

Henry Adams

MS HL

1. Printed in Ford, ed., *Letters of Henry Adams (1892–1918)*, 495, and Levenson
*et al.*, eds., *Letters of Henry Adams*, VI, 136.

2. *The Education of Henry Adams,* privately printed in Washington, D.C., in 1907, was not published until after Adams' death. Houghton Mifflin of Boston brought it out in 1918.

3. *Mont-Saint-Michel and Chartres,* a copy of which Adams had sent James in 1906.

## 27 JAMES TO ADAMS

3. Place des Etats-
   Unis
[Paris]
May 8*th* 1908.[1]

My dear Henry

I am kept here in gilded chains, in gorgeous bondage, in breathless attendance & luxurious *asservissement*—otherwise I should have acknowledged sooner your magnificent & magnanimous bounty. I am deeply & proudly grateful—& I promise myself an experience of the rarest quality as soon as I sit down to you in calmer conditions than these or than those I shall *immediately* find on my return (tomorrow,) to England. My brother William & his wife are there— "Hibbert" lecturing at Oxford, & I shall have to be there—at Oxford—& in town with them, in a good deal of a social & other hurly-burly, the whole of the rest of this month & doubtless a little of June—after which they will come down to stay with me in the country. All that will not make for the devout & concentrated communion with you of which I dream—but I shall defy the Fates, all the same, to keep me from getting at you more or less—& I foresee that I shall be borne aloft on billows of ecstatic comment. But of these things you shall hear from yours all constantly & gratefully

Henry James

P.S. I take the liberty of suggesting that you remain not too unaware of the fact that my hostess here, who has been reading you with a great overflow of delight, entertains for you such sentiments as will make any attention or attendance you may be able to render a thing of joy to her![2]

MS MHS

1. Printed in Edel, ed., *Henry James Letters*, IV, 490–91.

2. The hostess was Edith Wharton; what she must have been reading was Adams' *Education*.

## 28   JAMES TO ADAMS

Lamb House, Rye,
Sussex.
August 31*st* 1909.

My dear Henry!

I hear to day from Mrs. Wharton of the miserable & deplorable extinction of dear Bay Lodge, &, carrying my thoughts to you, very strongly, as the horrible event does, it causes the cup of my contrition for my long & damnable silence (ever since you did a very handsome thing by me 15 or 16 months ago) exceedingly—& bitterly—to overflow.[1] I know nothing of the circumstances of the miserable matter—no other echo of it having reached me; & it affects me as so odious & unnatural that my imagination supplies me with no easy hypothesis. But I have of him the most charming impression & recollection—I immensely liked him & felt the pity of not seeing more of him; & as it was mainly in your house I did see him I think of you as wretchedly wounded and deprived, & am moved to tell you of my cordial participation.

I recall him as so intelligent & open & delightful—a great & abundant social luxury; & the sense of how charming & friendly to me he was, in Washington, five years ago abides with me & touches me still. I don't like to think of his "people"—but you will know the pain & the difficulty of that far better than I; & will have to do it much, & see all the rest of the story through, "like" it as little as you may. And so I'm sorry to have to leave you unaided![2]

Yes, my long silence has been damnable, but vain explanations are more so; & I spare you the brave array of them that I have been saving up for you—spare you them even now when I have most need of them. *You* haven't, I feel—nor any use for them, & I must go down to history as graceless—& in truth *only* for having been so in such excess. You gave me your admirable & intensely interesting Book—or did you only commit it temporarily to my keeping?[3] I value it & am proud of the possession of it in too great a degree not to cling to the advantage of my doubt; but I hold it at your disposition on any slightest sign made. I speak of the reasons for my ugly dumbness as many, but they really all come back to my having been left by you with the crushing consciousness of far too much to say. I lost myself in your ample page as in a sea of memories & visions & associations—I dived *deep,* & I think felt your extraordinary element, every inch of its suggestion & recall & terrible thick evocation, so much that I have remained below, as it were, sticking fast in it even as an indiscreet fly in amber. Which is a figure but for saying that no reader of your band will have lived with you more responsively than yours all faithfully

                                                            *Henry James*

MS MHS

    1. George Cabot "Bay" Lodge (1873–1909), whose *Herakles* was published in November, 1908, died on August 21, 1909.
    2. To Elizabeth Cameron on September 4, 1909, Adams wrote: "I was cheered by a letter from Henry James about Bay Lodge, with the usual delightful largeness of expression:—'I recall him as so intelligent and open and delightful,—a great and abundant social luxury.' No one but James can make such strokes of the pen. Bay was indeed a social luxury *s'il en fut,* but, for that matter, so is Harry James too, and so are we all,—only not great or abundant" (Ford, ed., *Letters of Henry Adams (1892–1918),* 522n). At the behest of the Lodge family, Adams wrote *The Life of George Cabot Lodge,* a small volume brought out anonymously by Houghton Mifflin in 1911.
    3. James refers to Adams' privately printed *Education.*

## 29  ADAMS TO JAMES

                                                      23 Avenue du Bois
                                                        de Boulogne
                                                      [Paris]
                                                      Sept. 3. 1909[1]

My dear Friend
    Your letters, few as they are, have always the charm of saying something that carries one over the gaps; and when you describe

Bay Lodge as a great and abundant social luxury, you paint a portrait rather more lifelike than anything Sargent ever did. You paint even a group, for I believe we are all now social luxuries, and, as for myself, I am much flattered if regarded as bric-à-brac of a style,—dix-huitième by preference, rather than early Victorian. Nothing matters much! Only our proper labels! Please stick mine on, in your wonderfully perfect way, and I will sit quiet on the shelf, contented, among the rest.

As for what the newspapers report as the realities of life, I grow everyday too detached to feel them, and as for the volume you mention—which I did, in fact, at one time, mean to recall in order to give it completion of form,—I do not care what is done with it, as long as I do nothing myself. Bay Lodge's experience last winter completed and finished my own. When his Heracles appeared absolutely unnoticed by the literary press, I regarded my thesis as demonstrated—Society no longer shows the intellectual life necessary to enable it to react against a stimulus. My brother Brooks insists on the figure of paralysis.[2] I prefer the figure of diffusion, like that of a river falling into an ocean. Either way, it downed Bay, and has left me still floating, with vast curiosity to see what vaster absence of curiosity can bring about in my Sargasso sea.

Mrs. Wharton, in spite of her feminine energy and interest, is harder hit, I think, than I by the loss of Bay Lodge, but she has, besides, a heavy anxiety to face in the uncertainties of her husband's condition.[3] We are altogether a dilapidated social show, bric-à-brac or old-clo' shop, and I find smiling a rather mandarin amusement. Mrs. Wharton has told you about it, no doubt, but she will not have cared to dwell on it. My most immediate anxiety is Sturgis Bigelow, whose condition is very alarming to my shattered nervous system; but there are a dozen more such, in my close neighborhood, and Bay's catastrophe makes the solidest stars reel.[4]

I speculate occasionally on your doings and interests, and those of your fellow Englishmen, if you have fellows still; and I have even gone so far as to ask such insects as return, from time to time, after penetrating the hive,—Mrs. Wharton, the Ralph Curtis's, Berenson, and such,—what they have found in the way of wax or honey to store or consume, leaving small particles for me;[5] but the sad heart of Ruth was nothing worth mentioning, compared with the small crop of gleanings that I have effected among that alien corn. As usual, I got more active information from Berenson than from all the rest, and yet Berenson,—well! Berenson belongs to the primitives.

God be with you, all the same! though I associate only with aviators, and talk of the north pole with proper scepticism.[6]

*Ever yrs*
*Henry Adams*

MS HL

1. Printed in Ford, ed., *Letters of Henry Adams (1892–1918),* II, 522–23; Arvin, ed., *Selected Letters of Henry Adams,* 258–60; and Levenson *et al.,* eds., *Letters of Henry Adams,* VI, 269–70.
2. Brooks Adams (1848–1927), Henry's younger brother, published his ideas in several books, but most notably in *The Law of Civilization and Decay* (1895).
3. Edith's husband Edward "Teddy" Wharton suffered from deep depression and other, possibly psychosomatic, ills.
4. William Sturgis Bigelow (1850–1926) was Mrs. Henry Adams' cousin.
5. Adams refers to Ralph Wormeley Curtis (1854–1922) and Lise Colt Curtis, and also to Bernhard Berenson (1865–1959), art critic, connoisseur, and builder of collections (on commission), the best known of which, perhaps, is Isabella Gardner's Fenway Court.
6. Adams' reference is to Robert Edwin Peary (1856–1920), the American explorer who was credited with reaching the North Pole on April 6, 1909. His claim that he was the first to do so was disputed, however, and the controversy over primacy would stretch out over years. It is now doubted that he ever reached the North Pole.

### 30  ADAMS TO JAMES

1603 H Street
[Washington, D.C.]
22 January, 1911.[1]

My dear James

I did not write to you about your brother William, because I fancied that letters were a burden to you.[2] The other reason is that I felt the loss myself rather too closely to talk about it. We all began together, and our lives have made more or less of a unity, which is, as far as I can see, about the only unity that American society in our time had to show. Nearly all are gone. Richardson and St. Gaudens, LaFarge, Alex Agassiz, Clarence King, John Hay, and at the last, your brother William; and with each, a limb of our own lives cut off.[3] Exactly why we should be expected to talk about it, I don't know.

Meanwhile, as my time was too short in New York a week ago, I write to ask whether you do not mean to pay Washington a visit. I keep this hotel of mine open to guests until about the middle or the 10th of April. Except about ten days at the 22d February, I am still unoccupied. You can come by the first train, which would be best for my pleasure, or you can wait to please yourself. Washington is deadly dull, and gloomy beyond my experience, but that suits us well enough, and I can't say that Paris, when I left it, was any gayer. Mrs. Wharton remained there almost alone.

Come, then, at once, for a month!

*Ever yrs*
*Henry Adams*

MS HL

1. Printed with ellipses in Ford, ed., *Letters of Henry Adams (1892–1918)*, 558, and Levenson *et al.*, eds., *Letters of Henry Adams*, VI, 406–407.
2. William James, who was born in 1842, died on August 26, 1910, at Chocorua, New Hampshire.
3. Henry Hobson Richardson (1838–1886), architect; Augustus Saint-Gaudens (1848–1907), sculptor; John La Farge (1835–1910), artist; Alexander Agassiz (1835–1910), naturalist and scientist; Clarence King (1842–1901), geologist; and John Hay (1838–1905), diplomat and writer.

## 31  JAMES TO ADAMS

21, East Eleventh
Street.
New York.
January 26*th* 1911.

My dear Henry.

I greatly appreciate your kind letter & respond gratefully to what you say about our so full & proved & tested, our so *felt* con-

temporaneity, our so prolonged intercommunications of consciousness, so to speak—meaning by "us" my beloved Brother & you & I
& others of our so interesting generation whom you will name
without my help—even in addition to those you do name. I really
do feel like a lone Watcher of the Dead with you—& fully understand how you were moved quite *not* to break into loud articula-
tion when another, & even our so precious W. J., was added to the
number.[1]

To your liberal hospitality I also gratefully respond—if you will
allow me to take action to that effect a few weeks hence. Would *about*
the 15th March be convenient to you?—taking your own good time
to say, as it doesn't at all press. I should be delighted to come to you
for 3 or 4 days "some time along there."

And there is another matter, which this enclosed note from my
sister-in-law will doubtless sufficiently explain.[2] She gave it to me
just before I came on here to spend 2 or 3 weeks with the admirable
lady of this house[3]—that is she then sought your address of me, & I
told her that I believed you to be then here & that I should probably
see you & be able to deliver it. You had unfortunately departed,
however, by the hour I arrived—& my intention of immediately
writing to you *with* the accompanying, has been frustrated by the
complications of this unspeakable place—wild waters that for the
time closed over the head of yours all-faithfully

*Henry James*

P.S. On second thought, I post my sister's letter *with* this, but
separately.[4]
P.S. The letter to you that my sister speaks of *was* practically my
Brother's very last letter that wasn't a mere personal few words.

MS MHS

1. William James.
2. Alice James was his brother William's widow.
3. Mary Cadwalader Jones.
4. Henry James's "sister" was of course his sister-in-law.

## 32 ADAMS TO JAMES

1603 H Street
[Washington]
27 Jan. 1911.[1]

My dear James

I had hoped that Mrs. Jones would have packed you up, and personally conducted you here by the next train, but one must never put one's trust in women even when one can trust no one else.[2] She alone could have taken good care of you, and a few weeks here would soothe you both; but now I suppose you will have to arrange with Beatrix to bring you on, when she comes in March to do her term as Social Secretary for me.[3] Various people, from H. R. M.'s representative James Brice downwards are clamoring for you, and if you find my hotel unsatisfactory, I will move you about till you are suited.[4] I think mine the best, provided my Social Secretaries are on duty.

As for the world, I am done with it, and have no relations with it, and know nobody in it; but plenty of your friends and admirers will show you whatever exists, and protect you from the throng.

I have already attended to your sister-in-law's wish, and have sent her all the letters your brother wrote me in the last five years. They are but three or four.

*Ever truly yrs*
*Henry Adams*

MS HL

1. Printed in J. C. Levenson *et al.*, eds., *Supplement to "The Letters of Henry Adams": Letters Omitted from the Harvard University Press Edition of "The Letters of Henry Adams"* (Boston, 1989), Pt. 2.

2. Mrs. Jones was Mary Cadwalader Jones.

3. Beatrix Cadwalader Jones Farrand (1872–1959), Mrs. Cadwalader Jones's daughter and Edith Wharton's niece.

4. James Bryce (1838–1922) was at the time the British ambassador to the United States.

Henry Adams in the mid-1870s
*Courtesy Massachusetts Historical Society*

Henry James in 1883
*Courtesy John Hay Library, Brown University.* Reprinted from *Century Magazine*, November, 1882.

Henry and Clover Adams at Wenlock Abbey in 1873. Henry is standing at the left, and Clover is at the right. The others are Lady Pellington, Lady Cunliffe, Charles Milnes Gaskell, Sir Robert Cunliffe, and Lord Pellington.
*Courtesy Massachusetts Historical Society*

Marian "Clover" Hooper at Beverly Farms, Massachusetts, in 1869
*Courtesy Massachusetts Historical Society*

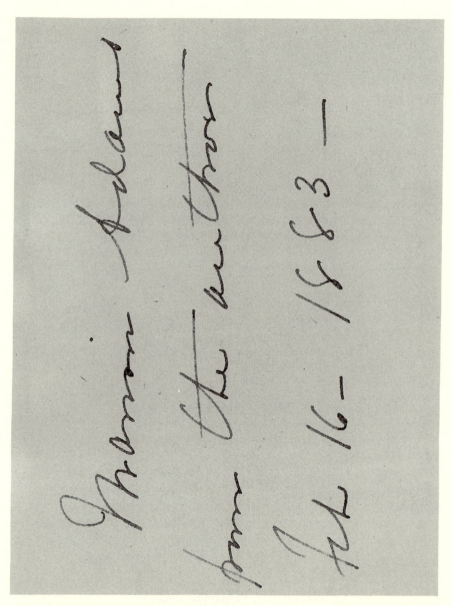

Inscription in Henry James's presentation copy of *The Siege of London* to Mrs. Henry Adams. It is in her handwriting.
*Courtesy Massachusetts Historical Society*

Portrait of Henry James by Jacques-Emile Blanche, 1908
*Courtesy National Portrait Gallery, Smithsonian Institution, Washington, D.C.*

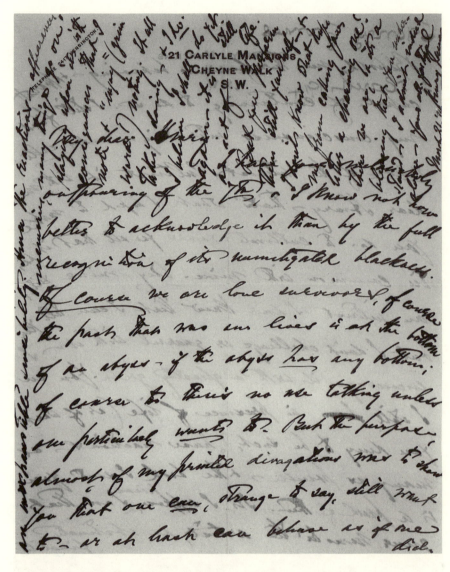

Manuscript page of James's letter to Adams, March 21, 1914
*Courtesy Massachusetts Historical Society*

Drawing of Henry Adams by John Briggs Potter, 1914
*Courtesy Massachusetts Historical Society*

## 33  JAMES TO ADAMS

Lamb House, Rye.
[Sussex]
July 15th, 1912[1]

My dear Henry.

I have heard of your sad trouble & I think of you with deep & tender participation.[2] Mrs. Cameron has been my main & most trusted source of knowledge, & has in a manner given me leave to tap at your more or less guarded door.[3] Of this I have the more promptly availed myself as I was already (as I intimate) hovering much about it, very near it, & weighing the discretion of my venturing to ask for admittance. That may have been wrong—& yet I stand by the fondness of my desire that some echo of my voice of inquiry & fidelity shall somehow reach you. In these great stresses friendship reaches out to the making of an image of the friend who has suffered assault—& I make one of you thus according to my sense of your rich & ingenious mind & your great resources of contemplation, speculation, resignation—a curiosity in which serenity is yet at home. I see you in short receive tribute of all your past, & at the same time but keep your future waiting to render you the same, or something very like it. Even if this evocation doesn't strike you as hitting the remark please believe that for me it does a great deal, & I require what I can get—so I give myself to the confidence. Upwards of three years ago I had a very grave illness, for which I had long been spoiling & from which I have long been incompletely emerging; I have now light on these things, I am an authority (really one of the rarest, I think;) & while I build myself up again, or do my best to, I draw you, by your leave, into the same course of treatment. May my devoted attention thus all soothingly, & not at all importunately, rest on you! I spent a year ago a twelvemonth in America—a very difficult & rather dreadful time—without seeing you, I know; but that was because I was unfit for adventures—condemned to hang far below the high pitch of Washington. I saw, alas, very little (& as regards persons very few,) that were propitious to my state—& I departed with an overwhelmed sense of having no nook or corner there. The whole scene struck me indeed as unfavorable to nooks—& I hied me back to *this* one, which more or less corresponds to the idea.—But I've spent the whole past winter in London—only lately returning thence, & even there I seemed to find more of a frame & a *fond*. There I saw again after something like 25 years poor Carlo Gaskell; looking very ill & very sad, altogether altered & perceptibly (save the mark!) "improved"—in the sense I mean of being gentler, softer, kinder. He was a strange old-world apparition—& it was stranger still to me that I had once, years ago, felt him contemporary! Lady Cattie is terrible—she has shed, by the dull wayside, every grace—of human garniture; & the thought that *that* (of old) had been the term of *this* struck me as again a theme for the moralist.[4] Then there was a young daughter—who was as absolute nought. It was a whole grim impression—including Everard Doyle; & I afterwards almost wept over it on the bosom of Gwynllian Palgrave, dear thing, a good friend of mine (the youngest of Frank's daughters) & quite the most sympathetic bit of wreckage of all that particular little circle of the other years.[5] But I should add that Carlo G. projected himself—with great concern into all newses & echoes of you. I just hear from Edith Wharton that she motors over hither from Paris a few days hence, & will spend 3 nights under my roof; which I bless because, with other reasons, I shall be able to talk of you with her.[6] Think of me as infinitely & insistently so disposed, & believe me, my dear Henry, all faithfully yours

*Henry James*

MS MHS

1. Printed in Robert F. Sayre, *The Examined Self: Benjamin Franklin, Henry Adams, Henry James* (Princeton, 1964), 186–88.

2. After suffering a first stroke on April 24, 1912, Adams had a relapse that lasted until mid-June (see Ernest Samuels, *Henry Adams: The Major Phase* [Cambridge, Mass., 1964], 533–36).

3. James refers to Elizabeth S. Cameron.

4. In this passage James refers to Charles Milnes Gaskell and his wife, Lady Catherine Gaskell.

5. Everard Hastings Doyle (1852–1933) was the son of Francis and Sidney Doyle. Gwenllian F. Palgrave published *Francis Turner Palgrave: His Journals and Memories of His Life* in 1899.

6. In his pocket diary under the date of July 21, 1912 (a Sunday), James wrote: "Edith Wharton arrived by her motor-car from Paris—to stay till Tuesday." Two

days later he noted that "Edith Wharton left 11 a.m." (Edel and Powers, eds., *Note-books*, 364).

## 34 JAMES TO ADAMS

> 21, Carlyle
> Mansions,
> Cheyne Walk. S. W.
> [London]
> May 26*th* 1913.[1]

My dear Henry!

It is long, much too long, that I have been owing you some expression of the extreme pleasure I have taken all these months in your magnificent rally (by all I hear,) from your sharp illness of last year. I began to want to rejoice with you over it from the moment of my getting from you the so benevolent letter which first gave me the clear image of it; but the case was, all too sadly, that about in the measure in which you found yourself so unerringly again, I went down, & still more down, like the other bucket in the well—quite out of the bottom of which dank & dusky shaft I should have felt I was calling up to you till a very short time since. I have had a diffi-cult & hampered winter—very much so indeed—after an all but im-possible autumn; but a persistent effort to emulate your gallantry, keeping it all the while steadily & shiningly before me, appears at last to be bearing some fruit. Take this belated "answer" to your ad-mirable last as a sign of what your example is helping me to. It helps me particularly as vividly & gratefully portrayed by dear little Ruth Draper, who kindly came to keep me company this a.m., thereby kindling a tender light in my poor old bedimmed countenance while I gave Sargent his 3d sitting for the portrait he is by a fantastic turn of the wheel of fate (*his* fate above all) doing of me.[2] He likes his sitter to be enlivened, & to provide therefore, & Ruth is (in the most exquisite way,) a positively professional enlivener. She is in fact hav-ing in that character the most rapid & acclaimed success here—something of which she will have told you. But she will have under-stated it, & the rate at which it goes (she performs this week for the

*third* time, I believe, at the Prss. Christian's) makes me greatly regret
that she sails for home again as soon as that is over. She would carry
everything before her for all June if she would but stick fast—as she
greatly wants to—but she feels, & I am afraid may be—for she alas
rather looks it—not well, & one hesitates, on that ground, to bully
her into boldness. She is the only star, I fear, that I can help to twin-
kle back at you. I came up from the country hither at the New Year
(in physical ease that made even that move rather a sad scramble:) &
I depart again on July 1st. But it's literally but the change from the
blue bed to the brown, & such exploits as your crossing of the sea &
re-installing & re-adventuring make me grovel before you even as
pale compromise before flushed triumph. I feel that I shall never
again quit this agitated island. I met 3 weeks (about) ago your
brother Charles, whom I had, oddly enough, never before encountered—& felt that he was contributing in no small degree to its agi-
tation.[3] I mean that I gathered him to have delivered an address (at
one of the meetings or banquets of the Historical Congress) which
had had a great retentissement. But of course you know all about
that—& at the George Trevelyan's Sunday afternoon, where I met
him, he enlivened my sitting as much as Ruth the charming did so
this morning in the studio.[4] I published some weeks ago the most
impudent volume that ever saw the light—an invitation to the world
to be regaled on the interesting emotions & reflections of its *serviteur*
from his 1st or 2d year to about his 16th—but such as it is I shld. like
to send it to you—now that I have an address for the purpose—if
you haven't happened to see it or become possessed of it.[5] Make me
that negative sign in 3 words, & you shall instantly have it. But
make me none other, I beg you—for I myself fear daily more &
more the weight of postal matter—I mean of the despatch of it, not
of the receipt. So with that fellow-feeling I let my correspondents
off easily—especially at this temperature, for we are having the torrid maximum, & I write you this at 11:30 p.m.—in my shirt-
sleeves, with big windows wide open to the river (which is a general
joy), a draught vainly sought by means of the open door. Were I to
permit myself a question other than the one just above I should ask
of you what has become of Edith Wharton—after all these
months—& whether she is back in Paris. But I forbid myself & feel
that it's in her being back in London that I am most interested. Let

me add that a very charming thing happened to me here the other day—or week—the signs & tokens of which will, I feel, amuse you (in the noblest sense of the word).[6] So I am sending them on with the earnest blessing of yours all faithfully

Henry James

MS MHS

1. Printed with ellipses in Sayre, *The Examined Self,* 189–90.
2. Ruth Draper (1884–1956), an American performer, was famous for her monologues, one of which James wrote (see "Three Unpublished Letters and a Monologue by Henry James," *London Mercury,* VI [September, 1922], 492–501). "I am sitting to [John Singer] Sargent for my portrait," James wrote to Jocelyn Persse on May 18, 1913, "that is I began today, and have the next sitting on Thursday next 22d. He *likes* one to have a friend there to talk with and to be talked to by, while he works—for animation of the countenance etc." (Edel, ed., *Henry James Letters,* IV, 671–72). The Sargent portrait had an interesting immediate history. In *Aspects and Impressions* (New York, 1922) Edmund Gosse writes: "He [James] sat, on the occasion of his seventieth birthday, to Mr. Sargent for the picture which is now one of the treasures of the National Portrait Gallery; this was surprisingly mutilated, while being exhibited at the Royal Academy, by a 'militant suffragette'; Henry James was extraordinarily exhilarated by having been thus 'impaired by the tomahawk of the savage,' and displayed himself as 'breasting a wondrous high-tide of postal condolence in this doubly-damaged state.' This was his latest excitement before the war with Germany drowned every other consideration" (p. 49).
3. Charles Francis Adams, Jr. (1835–1915), one of his three brothers, collaborated with Henry Adams on *Chapters of Erie, and Other Essays* (1871), an exposé of corruption.
4. George Otto Trevelyan (1838–1928), English historian and politician, held posts under W. E. Gladstone and was the author of *The Life and Letters of Lord Macaulay* (2 vols., 1876) and *The American Revolution* (6 vols., 1899–1914).
5. The volume was *A Small Boy and Others* (New York, 1913).
6. According to Sayre, the signs and token of that "very charming thing," a commemoration of James's seventieth birthday on April 15, 1913, were, as the result of a subscription by 250 friends, the gift of a "golden bowl," and the commissioning of the James portrait by Sargent. "A copy of the accompanying 'Letter,' with its long column of signers, and of James' reply was enclosed" with this letter from James to Adams (Sayre, *The Examined Self,* 191).

## 35 ADAMS TO JAMES

6, Square du Bois de
   Boulogne
[Paris]
29 May, 1913.[1]

My dear Friend

Your letter reminds me that it is just a year since I again woke
up, after an eternity of unconsciousness, to this queer mad world,
ten times queerer and madder than ever, and what a vast gulf opened
to me between the queerness of the past and the total inconsequence
of the present. The gulf has not closed: it is rather wider today than a
year ago; but I wake up every morning and I go to sleep every night
with a stronger sense that each day is an isolated fact, to be taken by
itself and looked at as a dance. Our friend Ruth helped me, and I am
glad to think that she helped you. We need it. I take all the help I can
get, and hang on to it with a grip that really does me credit. I am
sorry to say that men are no good. They are wretched imbeciles in
carrying their fellows. Only women are worth cultivating, and I am
ready to hand over the whole universe to them if they want it,—
though I fail to conceive why they should want such a preposterous
absurdity. They can't even make it more absurd than it is, which
must be a sad thought to them, considering how successful the men
have been in absurdifying the women.

Probably you are not yet old enough to enjoy this point of view.
After all, you are but a boy,—only seventy. I have all your septuani-
sation, you know. Had I come over in time, I should have been on
your list; as it is, I got it all from the Walter Gays.[2] On the sea, I had
three nieces reading to me your infancy, and I left in New York all
your friends racing to put down their names—and mine—on your
roll of American adherents. You stopped us, it seems, after I sailed,
but we were all there, pretty girls and matrons and old sages.

Edith Wharton got back here and has promptly gone to bed. She
promises to get up. Of course I know nothing of my brother
Charles except that he was seen in a dishevelled condition flying
from Eustis Square. He and I differ widely about railway journeys. I

do not know his opinions about less important matters. He cares nothing for my 12th century songs, and is even cold to my 30,000-year-old babies and other citizens, which is fatal to brotherly affection.

I am more concerned about Mrs. Cameron who is now in London with Martha, trying to find out whether anything is the matter with Martha which will explain her last collapse since returning from Egypt.[3] We elderly people are just old, but the young ones beat us even on our own strong point,—they are older.

As for me, I care only for my friends.[4] Write again soon.

> *Ever yrs*
> *Henry Adams*

MS HL

1. Printed with ellipses in Ford, ed., *Letters of Henry Adams (1898–1918)*, 612–13, and Levenson *et al.*, eds., *Letters of Henry Adams*, VI, 602–603.
2. Walter Gay (1856–1937), an American art collector, and his wife Matilda Travers Gay (1856–1943).
3. Martha Cameron (Lindsay) was Elizabeth Cameron's daughter.
4. When William Roscoe Thayer, who was preparing a biography of John Hay, wrote to ask for Adams' help, Adams answered him on December 26, 1913: "Such ambition as I retain has of late years been directed to creating round my group of friends a certain atmosphere of art and social charm. They were not numerous, but were all superior. John LaFarge, Alex Agassiz, Clarence King, St. Gaudens, Hay, and their more-or-less close associates like Bret Harte, John Sargent, Henry James, &c, &c, were distinguished men in any time or country. John Hay alone was a public character, and needs separate treatment. I am glad you have undertaken him" (Levenson *et al.*, eds., *Letters of Henry Adams*, VI, 629).

## 36  JAMES TO ADAMS

> 21 Carlyle Mansions
> Cheyne Walk S. W.
> [London]
> March 21. '14.[1]

My dear Henry

I have your melancholy outpouring of the *7th*, & I know not how to acknowledge it than by the full recognition of its unmitigated blackness.[2] *Of course* we are lone survivors, of course the past that was our lives is at the bottom of an abyss—if the abyss *has* any bottom; of course too there's no use talking unless one particularly *wants* to. But the purpose, almost, of my printed divagations was to show you that one *can,* strange to say, still want to—or at least can behave as if one did. Behold me therefore so behaving—& apparently capable of continuing to do so. I still find my consciousness interesting—under *cultivation* of the interest. Cultivate it *with* me, dear Henry—that's what I hoped to make you do; to cultivate yours for all that it has in common with mine. *Why* mine yields an interest I don't know that I can tell you, but I don't challenge or quarrel with it—I encourage it with a ghastly grin. You see I still, in presence of life (or of what you deny to be such,) have reactions—as many as possible—& the book I sent you is a proof of them. It's, I suppose, because I am that queer monster the artist, an obstinate finality, an inexhaustible sensibility. Hence the reactions—appearances, memories, many things go on playing upon it with consequences that I note & "enjoy" (grim word!) noting. It all takes doing—& I *do*. I believe I shall do yet again—it is still an act of life. But you perform them still yourself—& I don't know what keeps me from calling your letter a charming one! There we are, & it's a blessing that you understand—I admit indeed alone—your all-faithful

*Henry James*[3]

MS MHS

1. Printed in Lubbock, ed., *Letters of Henry James,* II, 360–61; F. O. Matthiessen, *The James Family* (New York, 1947), 669; Leon Edel, ed., *Selected Letters of Henry James* (New York, 1955), 173–74; Sayre, *The Examined Self,* 193; Edel, ed., *Henry James Letters,* IV, 705–706; and Edel, ed., *Selected Letters of Henry James* (1987), 419–20.

2. Adams' letter has not survived. Something of its contents can be inferred, however, from Adams' letter to Elizabeth Cameron on March 8, 1914: "I've read Henry James's last bundle of memories [*Notes of a Son and Brother* (1914)] which have reduced me to dreary pulp. Why did we live? Was that all? Why was I not born in Central Africa and died young. Poor Henry James thinks it all real, I believe, and actually still lives in that dreamy, stuffy Newport and Cambridge, with papa James and Charles Norton—and me! Yet, why! It is a terrible dream, but not so wierd as this here which is quite loony. Never mind!" (Levenson *et al.,* eds., *Letters of Henry Adams,* VI, 638).

3. A quite different response to James's *Notes of a Son and Brother* is that of

Oliver Wendell Holmes. In a letter to Lewis Einstein on April 17, 1914, Holmes writes: "I have listened while playing solitaire to portions of H. James's second autobiographical volume. He gives the impression that he seeks to, in spite of his style, which shows that the medium does not matter if you can do the trick. I mention it because it recalls the time when we were intimate. I knew well Minnie Temple some of whose remarkable letters he prints (she died young) and his father whose letters are perhaps the most vivid things in the book. It recalled the total impression of the family, with its moral refinement, its keen personal intuitions, the optimistic anarchising of the old man, (a spiritual, unpractical anarchism) its general go-as-you-please but demand-nothing, apotheotic Irishry. One had to invent a word to hit it" (James Bishop Peabody, ed., *Holmes-Einstein Letters: Correspondence of Mr. Justice Holmes and Lewis Einstein, 1903–1935* [London, 1964], 89–90).

# APPENDIX
## Calendar of Unlocated Letters

Information contained in existing letters indicates that there was additional correspondence between Henry James and Henry Adams other than what is now extant. The following list identifies the unlocated letter by author, addressee, and probable date, followed by the reference to the missing correspondence and the source of that reference. This list is undoubtedly incomplete, for only items of high probability have been included.

HJ to HA
January, 1877

"This, meanwhile, is only to acknowledge & thank you for your packet [of letters of introduction], which arrived this a.m. Your picture of Boston . . ."
HJ to HA, January 13, [1877]

HA to HJ
July, 1877

"Just before I left London came to me your letter . . ."
HJ to HA, July 15, [1877]

"a letter from H. Adams saying—'If Gaskell asks you to Wenlock don't for the world fail to go'; and adding other remarks, of a most attractive kind"
HJ to William James, July 10, 1877
(Edel, ed., *Henry James Letters,* II, 123)

HA to HJ
April, 1879

"I am delighted to hear of the prospect of your so soon turning up on this side of the globe. . . . your letter, this a.m. received, imparts reality to the vision."
HJ to HA, May 5, [1879]

Appendix


MA to HJ
September, 1880

"Your favour just received."

HJ to MA, September 9, [1880]


MA to HJ
November, 1881

"the gracious note I received from your wife just after despatching her an . . . not less gracious one, three or four (five or six) weeks ago."

HJ to HA, December 20, 1881


HA to HJ
December, 1881

"Thank you for your Castilian offers!"

HJ to HA, December 27, 1881


MA to HJ
February, 1883

"It was very pleasant, the other day, to see your hand-writing . . ."

HJ to MA, February 28, [1883]


MA to HJ
February, 1885

"Your rustic note has the aroma of Lafayette Square . . ."

HJ to MA, March 9, [1885]


HA to HJ
June, 1892

"Lefautau's little letter is charming . . . and I thank you kindly for having transmitted it."

HJ to HA, June 15, [1892]

HA to HJ
October, 1895

"There was much I wanted to hear from you. Alas! Do try me again . . ."
HJ to HA [October (?) 1895]


HJ to HA
November, 1904

"Very noble and beautiful your letter . . ."
HJ to HA, November 24, 1904


HA to HJ
December, 1904

"I am in receipt of great benevolence from you—through, 1st, the grace of Mrs. Cameron, & 2d, that of your letter."
HJ to HA, December 23, 1904


HA to HJ
January, 1905

"Only a word to say that, yes, very positively & rejoicingly, I present myself at your door on Tuesday afternoon next 9th."
HJ to HA, January 7, 1905


HA to HJ
January, 1905

"I have written 1st to thank R. U. Johnson for crowning me with glory—& now I must thank *you* for guiding, straight to my unworthy & even slightly bewildered brow, his perhaps otherwise faltering or reluctant hand."
HJ to HA, February 1, 1905

Appendix

HA to HJ
July, 1906

"I grieve to read what you tell me of John LaFarge . . ."

HJ to HA, July 30, 1906

HA to HJ
July, 1907

"I am much touched by your kind letter"

HJ to HA, July 8, 1907

HA to HJ
April or May, 1908

"I am kept here in gilded chains . . . otherwise I should have acknowledged sooner your magnificent & magnanimous bounty."

HJ to HA, May 8, 1908

HA to HJ
(?) 1913

"Take this belated 'answer' to your admirable last . . ."

HJ to HA, May 26, 1913

HA to HJ
March 7, 1914

"I have your melancholy outpouring of the 7*th* . . ."

HJ to HA, March 21, 1914

# BIBLIOGRAPHY

## MANUSCRIPT COLLECTIONS

Adams, Henry. Papers. Massachusetts Historical Society, Boston.
Adams, Henry. Papers. Microfilm copy. Brown University, Providence, R.I.
Dwight, Theodore F. Papers. Massachusetts Historical Society, Boston.
Godkin, E. L. Papers. Houghton Library, Harvard University, Cambridge, Mass.
James, Henry. Collection (#6251). Clifton Waller Barrett Library, Manuscripts Division, Special Collections Department, University of Virginia Library, Charlottesville.
James Family Papers. Houghton Library, Harvard University, Cambridge, Mass.
Shattuck Collection. Massachusetts Historical Society, Boston.

## BOOKS AND ARTICLES CITED

Adams, Henry. *Democracy: An American Novel*. New York, 1880.
———. *The Education of Henry Adams*. Boston, 1918.
———. *The Life of Albert Gallatin*. Philadelphia, 1879.
———. *The Life of George Cabot Lodge*. Boston, 1911.
———. *Mont-Saint-Michel and Chartres*. Boston, 1913.
Adams, Henry, and Charles Francis Adams. *Chapters of Erie, and Other Essays*. Boston, 1871.
Arvin, Newton, ed. *Selected Letters of Henry Adams*. New York, 1951.
Cater, Harold Dean, ed. *Henry Adams and His Friends*. Boston, 1947.
Chanler, Mrs. Winthrop. *Roman Spring: Memoirs*. Boston, 1934.
Cox, John F., ed. "Some Letters of Thomas Woolner to Mr. and Mrs. Henry Adams [I]." *Journal of Pre-Raphaelite Studies*, I (May, 1981), 1–27.
Edel, Leon. *Henry James: The Conquest of London, 1870–1881*. Philadelphia, 1962.
———. *Henry James: The Master, 1901–1916*. Philadelphia, 1972.
———. *Henry James: The Middle Years, 1882–1895*. Philadelphia, 1962.
———. *Henry James: The Treacherous Years, 1895–1901*. Philadelphia, 1969.
———, ed. *The Diary of Alice James*. New York, 1964.
———, ed. *Henry James Letters*. 4 vols. Cambridge, Mass., 1974–84.

————, ed. *Selected Letters of Henry James*. New York, 1955.

————, ed. *Selected Letters of Henry James*. Cambridge, Mass., 1987.

Edel, Leon, and Lyall H. Powers, eds. *The Complete Notebooks of Henry James*. New York, 1987.

Eliot, T. S. "In Memory." *Little Review*, V (August, 1918), 44–47.

————. "A Sceptical Patrician" (unsigned review of *The Education of Henry Adams*). *Athenaeum*, May 23, 1919, pp. 361–62.

Eppard, Philip B. "Henry Adams and the Letters and Diaries of John Hay." *Books at Brown*, XXIX–XXX (1982–1983), 119–28.

Foley, Richard Nicholas. *Criticism in American Periodicals of the Works of Henry James from 1866–1916*. Washington, D.C., 1944.

Ford, Worthington Chauncey, ed. *Letters of Henry Adams (1892–1918)*. Boston, 1938.

Gosse, Edmund. *Aspects and Impressions*. New York, 1922.

Hardwick, Elizabeth, ed. *Selected Letters of William James*. New York, 1961.

Harlow, Virginia. *Thomas Sergeant Perry: A Biography*. Durham, N.C., 1950.

Hay, John. "James's *The Portrait of a Lady*" (unsigned review). New York *Tribune*, December 25, 1881, p. 8

James, Henry. "Abbeys and Castles." *Lippincott's Magazine*, XX (October, 1877), 434–42.

————. *The Art of the Novel: Critical Prefaces*. Edited by Richard P. Blackmur. New York, 1934.

————. *The Author of Beltraffio*. Boston, 1885.

————. *English Hours*. Edited by Alma Louise Lowe. New York, 1960.

————. *Notes of a Son and Brother*. New York, 1914.

————. "The Picture Season in London." *Galaxy*, XXIV (August, 1877), 149–61.

————. *The Portrait of a Lady*. Boston, 1881.

————. *The Siege of London, The Pension Beaurepas, and The Point of View*. Boston, 1883.

————. *A Small Boy and Others*. New York, 1913.

————. "Three Unpublished Letters and a Monologue by Henry James." *London Mercury*, VI (September, 1922), 492–501.

————. *William Wetmore Story and His Friends*. 2 vols. Boston, 1903.

La Farge, John. *Reminiscences of the South Seas*. New York, 1912.

La Farge (S.J.), John. "Henry James's Letters to the LaFarges." *New England Quarterly*, XXII (1949), 173–92.

*Letters of John Hay and Extracts from Diary*. 3 vols. Washington, D.C., 1908.

Levenson, J. C., *et al.*, eds. *The Letters of Henry Adams*. 6 vols. Cambridge, Mass., 1982–88.

————. *Supplement to "The Letters of Henry Adams": Letters Omitted from the Harvard University Press Edition of "The Letters of Henry Adams."* 2 pts. Boston, 1989.

Lubbock, Percy, ed. *The Letters of Henry James*. 2 vols. New York, 1920.

Matthiessen, F. O. *The James Family*. New York, 1947.

Monteiro, George. "A Contemporary View of Henry James and Oscar Wilde, 1882." *American Literature*, XXXV (1964), 528–30.

————. *Henry James and John Hay: The Record of a Friendship*. Providence, R.I., 1965.
————. "Henry James and the American Academy of Arts and Letters." *New England Quarterly*, XXXVI (March, 1963), 82–84.
————. "An Unpublished Henry James Letter." *Notes and Queries*, n.s., X (April, 1963), 143–44.
Moore, Charles. *The Life and Times of Charles Follen McKim*. Boston, 1929.
Palgrave, Gwenllian F. *Francis Turner Palgrave: His Journals and Memories of His Life*. London, 1899.
Peabody, James Bishop, ed. *Holmes-Einstein Letters: Correspondence of Mr. Justice Holmes and Lewis Einstein, 1903–1935*. London, 1964.
Perry, Ralph Barton, ed. *The Thought and Character of William James*. 2 vols. Boston, 1935.
Powers, Lyall H., ed. *Henry James and Edith Wharton: Letters, 1900–1915*. New York, 1990.
Richards, Bernard. "Henry James's 'Fawns.'" *Modern Language Studies*, XIII (Fall, 1983), 154–68.
Riley, Stephen T. "A Nugget from the Theodore F. Dwight Papers." *M.H.S. Miscellany*, no. 9 (1966), 1–2.
Samuels, Ernest. *Henry Adams: The Major Phase*. Cambridge, Mass., 1964.
Sayre, Robert F. *The Examined Self: Benjamin Franklin, Henry Adams, Henry James*. Princeton, 1964.
Sweeney, John L., ed. *The Painter's Eye: Notes and Essays on the Pictorial Arts by Henry James*. Cambridge, Mass., 1956.
Taylor, Linda J. *Henry James, 1866–1916: A Reference Guide*. Boston, 1982.
Tehan, Arline Boucher. *Henry Adams in Love: The Pursuit of Elizabeth Sherman Cameron*. New York, 1983.
Thoron, Ward, ed. *The Letters of Mrs. Henry Adams, 1865–1883*. Boston, 1936.
Wells, Kate Gannett. "Women in Organizations." *Atlantic Monthly*, XLVI (September, 1880), 360–67.

## THE JAMES-ADAMS RELATIONSHIP: ADDITIONAL SOURCES

Anderson, Quentin. *The American Henry James*. New Brunswick, N.J., 1957.
————. *The Imperial Self: An Essay in American Literary and Cultural History*. New York, 1971.
Auchincloss, Louis. *Henry Adams*. Minneapolis, 1971.
Blackmur, R. P. *Henry Adams*. Edited by Veronica A. Makowsky. New York, 1980.
————. "Henry Adams: Three Late Moments." *Kenyon Review*, II (Winter, 1940), 7–29.
Buitenhuis, Peter. *The Grasping Imagination: The American Writings of Henry James*. Toronto, 1970.
Byrnes, Joseph F. *The Virgin of Chartres: An Intellectual and Psychological History of the Work of Henry Adams*. Rutherford, N.J., 1981.

Cargill, Oscar. *The Novels of Henry James.* New York, 1961.

Donoghue, Denis. "The American Style of Failure." *Sewanee Review,* LXXXII (Summer, 1974), 407–32.

————. "Henry Adams' Novels." *Nineteenth Century Fiction,* XXXIX (September, 1984), 186–201.

Dupee, F. W. *Henry James.* New York, 1951.

Dusinberre, William. *Henry Adams: The Myth of Failure.* Charlottesville, Va., 1980.

Edel, Leon. *Henry James: A Life.* New York, 1985.

————. *Henry James: The Untried Years, 1843–1870.* Philadelphia, 1953.

Friedrich, Otto. *Clover.* New York, 1979.

Gale, Robert L. *A Henry James Encyclopedia.* New York, 1989.

————. "'Pandora' and Her President." *Studies in Short Fiction,* I (Spring, 1964), 222–24.

Harbert, Earl N. *The Force So Much Closer Home: Henry Adams and the Adams Family.* New York, 1977.

Hocks, Richard A. *Henry James and Pragmatistic Thought.* Chapel Hill, N.C., 1974.

Howe, Irving. Introduction to *The Bostonians,* by Henry James. New York, 1956.

Hume, Robert A. *Runaway Star: An Appreciation of Henry Adams.* Ithaca, N.Y., 1951.

Hyde, H. Montgomery. *Henry James at Home.* New York, 1969.

Jacobson, Marcia. *Henry James and the Mass Market.* University, Ala., 1983.

Jordy, William H. *Henry Adams: Scientific Historian.* New Haven, Conn., 1952.

Kaledin, Eugenia. *The Education of Mrs. Henry Adams.* Philadelphia, 1981.

Kraft, James. *The Early Tales of Henry James.* Carbondale, Ill., 1969.

Kreyling, Michael. "Nationalizing the Southern Hero: Adams and James." *Mississippi Quarterly,* XXXIV (Fall, 1981), 383–402.

Krook, Dorothea. *The Ordeal of Consciousness in Henry James.* Cambridge, Eng., 1962.

LeClair, Robert C. *Three American Travellers in England: James Russell Lowell, Henry Adams, Henry James.* Philadelphia, 1945.

Lee, Brian. *The Novels of Henry James.* London, 1978.

Levenson, J. C. *The Mind and Art of Henry Adams.* Boston, 1957.

Lewis, R. W. B. *The Jameses: A Family Narrative.* New York, 1991.

Leyburn, Ellen Douglas. *Strange Alloy: The Relation of Comedy to Tragedy in the Fiction of Henry James.* Chapel Hill, N.C., 1968.

Mane, Robert. *Henry Adams on the Road to Chartres.* Cambridge, Mass., 1971.

Matthiessen, F. O. *The Achievement of T. S. Eliot.* New York, 1935.

————. *Henry James: The Major Phase.* New York, 1944.

Matthiessen, F. O., and Kenneth B. Murdock, eds. *The Notebooks of Henry James.* New York, 1947.

Monteiro, George. "'He Do the Police in Different Voices': James's 'The Point of View.'" *Topic,* XXXVII (1983), 3–9.

————. "Henry Adams' Jamesian Education." *Massachusetts Review,* XXIX (Summer, 1988), 371–84.

————. "Washington Friends and National Reviewers: Henry James's 'Pandora.'" *Research Studies,* XLIII (March, 1975), 38–44.

Morison, Elting E., *et al.*, eds. *The Letters of Theodore Roosevelt.* Vol. VI of 8 vols. Cambridge, Mass., 1954.

Noble, James Ashcroft. "New Novels" (review of *Democracy*). *Academy,* XXII (July 1, 1882), 5.

Nuhn, Ferner. *The Wind Blew From the East: A Study in the Orientation of American Culture.* New York, 1942.

O'Toole, Patricia. *The Five of Hearts: An Intimate Portrait of Henry Adams and His Friends, 1880–1918.* New York, 1990.

Porter, Carolyn. *Seeing and Being: The Plight of the Participant Observer in Emerson, James, Adams, and Faulkner.* Middletown, Conn., 1981.

Rahv, Philip, ed. *Discovery of Europe.* Boston, 1947.

Rogat, Yosal. "The Judge as Spectator." *University of Chicago Law Review,* XXXI (Winter, 1964), 213–56.

Rovit, Earl. "James and Emerson: The Lesson of the Master." *American Scholar,* XXXIII (Summer, 1964), 434–40.

Rowe, John Carlos. *Henry Adams and Henry James.* Ithaca, N.Y., 1976.

Samuels, Ernest. *Henry Adams.* Cambridge, Mass., 1989.

————. *Henry Adams: The Middle Years.* Cambridge, Mass., 1958.

————. *The Young Henry Adams.* Cambridge, Mass., 1948.

Scheyer, Ernst. *The Circle of Henry Adams: Art & Artists.* Detroit, 1970.

Sicker, Philip. *Love and the Quest for Identity in the Fiction of Henry James.* Princeton, 1980.

Smit, David W. *The Language of a Master: Theories of Style and the Late Writings of Henry James.* Carbondale, Ill., 1988.

Stein, William Bysshe. "*The Portrait of a Lady:* Vis Inertiae." *Western Humanities Review,* XIII (Spring, 1959), 177–90.

Stevenson, Elizabeth. *Henry Adams: A Biography.* New York, 1955.

Stowell, H. Peter. *Literary Impressionism: James and Chekhov.* Athens, Ohio, 1980.

Tanner, Tony. "Henry James and Henry Adams." *Tri-Quarterly,* no. 11 (Winter, 1968), 91–108.

Trilling, Lionel. Introduction to *The Bostonians,* by Henry James. London, 1952.

Vandersee, Charles. "James's 'Pandora': The Mixed Consequences of Revision." *Studies in Bibliography,* XXI (1968), 93–108.

Ward, J. A. "Silence, Realism and 'The Great Good Place.'" *Henry James Review,* III (Winter, 1982), 129–32.

Welland, Dennis. "'Improvised Europeans': Thoughts on an Aspect of Henry James and T. S. Eliot." *Bulletin of the John Rylands University Library of Manchester,* LXVI (Autumn, 1983), 256–77.

Wilson, Edmund. *Patriotic Gore: Studies in the Literature of the American Civil War.* New York, 1962.

Winters, Yvor. *The Anatomy of Nonsense.* Norfolk, Conn., 1943.

Woodward, C. Vann. *The Burden of Southern History.* Rev. ed. Baton Rouge, 1968.

# INDEX

Alcott, Amos Bronson, 60, 61*n*3
Allen, Jessie, 23
American Academy of Arts and Letters, 25, 67–68*n*2, 68*n*4
American Girl: James on, 11, 12
American Man: Adams on, 25
American Woman: Adams on, 25, 26
American Institute of Architects, 65–66, 66*n*2, 70*n*3
Anderson, Mary, 55, 56*n*9
"Ann Eliza(s)," 7, 14
Appleton, Nathan, 7
Appleton, T. G., 7
Ariimanihinihi, 57, 57–58*n*1
Arnold, Matthew, 4
Arnold, Mrs. Matthew, 4
Arthur, Chester A.: James on, 11; mentioned, 12
*Atlantic Monthly,* xvi, 47*n*1

Balestier, Charles Wolcott: Adams on 18–19; mentioned, 17
Barrymore, Ethel, 25
Bayard, Katherine, 11, 53, 54*n*6, 55, 56*n*8
Bayard, Thomas Francis, 10, 54*n*6, 56*n*8
Beale, Emily (Mrs. John Roll McLean), 53, 54*n*6
Berenson, Bernhard, 28, 77, 78, 78*n*5
Bigelow, William Sturgis: Adams on, 77; mentioned, 78*n*4
Blackwood, William, 63*n*3
Blaine, James G., 10, 11
Blanche, Jacques-Emile: 27; portrait of Henry James, 27
Bonington, Richard Parkes, 36, 38*n*6
Boott, Elizabeth, 1, 3, 61*n*5
Boott, Francis, 60, 61*n*5
Boston *Daily Advertiser,* xv
Boston *Daily Courier,* xv
Bourget, Minnie (Mrs. Paul Bourget), 57, 58*n*2
Bourget, Paul, 57, 58*n*2
Brice, James. *See* Bryce, James

British Female, 5, 6
Bryce, James, 81, 81*n*4

Cameron, Donald, xx, 20, 21, 66*n*1
Cameron, Elizabeth: James on, 21–22; quoted, 31, 32; mentioned, xx, 14, 17, 18, 20, 21, 22, 23, 27, 29, 30, 31, 32, 65, 66*n*1, 66, 76*n*2, 82, 83*n*3, 89*n*2, 93
Cameron (Lindsay), Martha, 88, 88*n*3
Carter, Mrs., 47, 47*n*3
*Century Magazine,* xviii, 13, 14, 67*n*2
Chanler, Margaret: quoted, 24
Chiki, Miss, 57*n*1
Clark, Sir John Forbes, 6, 7, 11, 16, 17, 49*n*4, 52*n*3
Clark, Mary Temple Rose (Mrs. Stanley Clark), 55, 56*n*12
Clark, Colonel Stanley, 56*n*12
Cleveland, Grover, 55, 56*n*8
*Continental Monthly,* xvi
*Cornhill Magazine,* xvii
Cornwall, Barry (Waller Bryan Procter), 56*n*2
Cotman, John Sell, 36, 38*n*6
Cox, Judge Walter Smith, 49, 50*n*2
Crane, Stephen, 68*n*3
Crawford, Francis Marion: 14; *Mr. Isaacs,* 14
Cunliffe, Lady (Eleanor Sophia Egerton Leigh), 35, 37*n*2, 39, 40
Cunliffe, Sir Robert Alfred, 3, 5*n*7, 35, 37*n*2, 39, 40, 46*n*3, 55
Curtis, Lise Colt, 77, 78*n*5
Curtis, Ralph Wormeley, 77, 78*n*5

Darwin, Charles, 56*n*7
Darwin, Sara Sedgwick, 55, 56*n*7
Darwin, William, 55, 56*n*7
Daudet, Alphonse, 14
Dewolfe, Elsie, 25
Dickens, Charles, 14
Douglas, Alfred Lord, 19
Doyle, Everard Hastings, 83, 83*n*5